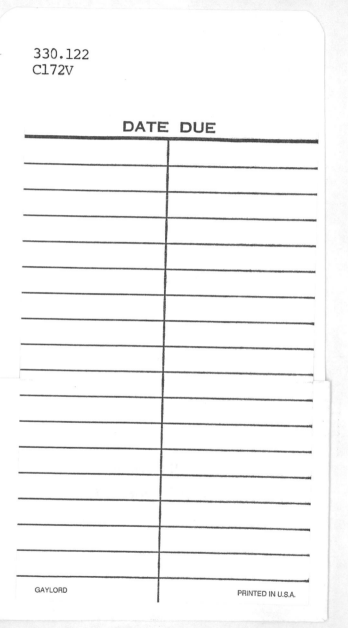

DATE DUE

Capitalism:
Sources
Of
Hostility

Capitalism:
Sources
Of
Hostility

edited by
Ernest van den Haag

Published by

 EPOCH BOOKS
NEW ROCHELLE, NEW YORK

for

Manufactured in the United States of America

Library of Congress Cataloging in Publication Data

Capitalism, sources of hostility.

CONTENTS: Van den Haag, E. Confusion, envy, fear, and longing.—Bauer, P. T. Hostility to the market in less developed countries.
—Glazer, N. Comment on P. T. Bauer's "Hostility to the market in
less developed countries." [etc.]

1. Capitalism—Addresses, essays, lectures.
I. Van den Haag, Ernest.
HB501.C2425   330.12′2   79-18151
ISBN 0-89948-000-4

Contents-

Contributors

Peter Bauer is Professor of Economics at the London School of Economics, and a Fellow of Gonville and Caius College, Cambridge University, as well as a Fellow of the British Academy. He is the co-author (with B.S. Yamey) of the classic work *The Economics of Under-Developed Countries,* and a regular contributor to scholarly journals on both sides of the Atlantic.

Lewis S. Feuer is University Professor of the Humanities and Social Sciences at the University of Virginia. He has taught at Harvard, the University of California at Berkeley, and the University of Toronto. His books include *The Conflict of Generations, Marx and the Intellectuals,* and *Ideology and the Ideologists.*

Nathan Glazer is Professor of Education and Sociology at Harvard University, and co-editor of *The Public Interest.* His books include *The Lonely Crowd* and *Faces in the Crowd* (both with David Riesman), *Beyond the Melting Pot* (with Daniel Patrick Moynihan), and *Affirmative Discrimination.*

Stanley Rothman is Professor of Sociology and of Government at Smith College. His publications include *European Society and Politics* and contributions to many scholarly journals.

Roger Starr is the former Commissioner of the New York City Housing and Development Administration, and the Henry Luce Professor of Urban Values at New York University. A member of the Board of Editors of *The New York Times*, he has published widely.

Ernest van den Haag, the editor, is a Visiting Professor of Criminal Justice at the State University of New York (Albany), and Professor of Law at the New York Law School. His Ph.D. is in economics and he also teaches sociology and psychology at the New School for Social Research. A practicing psychoanalyst and member of the Council on Foreign Relations (as well as the editorial board of *Policy Review*), he has published extensively in journals here and abroad. His most recent book is *Punishing Criminals.*

Dale Vree's most recent book is *Synthesizing Marxism and Christianity.* He is the Executive Editor of the *New Oxford Review* and Professor of Christian Social Ethics at the Anglican Theological College in Berkeley, California.

Introduction

According to Immanuel Kant the insane should be tutored by philosophers. The insane reason faultily, Kant argued. Therefore, he thought, experts in correct reasoning are most apt to help them. Tutored by philosophers the insane would learn to reason properly and thus become rational.

Since Kant's time we have learned that grossly defective reasoning and gross misperceptions of reality often are but symptoms of underlying emotional problems; this is usually so when the inaccurate perceptions and inferences are immune to factual evidence or logic. In such cases incorrect arguments must be considered primarily as symptoms. They yield to correct arguments only after the emotional need gratified by the symptom is gratified in some other way, or no longer felt. Symptoms arising from emotional needs or disturbances cannot be remedied by exhorting to rationality or by correcting erroneous reasoning. Counterarguments do not avail, nor does any intellectual instruction. This much has become common knowledge, although the etiological importance of emotions is more often accepted in theory than in practice.* Still, at least in theory, we now

*For instance, "sex education" is often advocated to cure or prevent irrational, illegitimate or unhealthy sexual behavior

find it more effective to inquire what makes disturbed persons act or think or feel as they do, to uncover the nonrational roots of their symptoms, rather than to merely exhort them to act reasonably, or to attempt to prove to them by argument how unreasonable or delusional they are. When the disturbance and the irrationality are obvious and when they are not widely shared or cloaked in rational arguments, we no longer believe in cure by argument. We no longer ask philosophers to tutor the insane. The importance of emotions has been accepted—sometimes even to the point of denigrating the role the intellect can play.

However, when it comes to less obvious and more widely shared distortions of reality, we often deal with them on a purely rational level, neglecting to ask ourselves what leads intelligent people to misperceive what goes on. Obviously such people—intelligent and convinced Nazis, or communists, are an extreme example—need not be sick. They need not suffer, or defeat themselves. They need not be less able than others to feel, reason or behave normally. Yet they misperceive a major part of social reality. (I do not have in mind those

---

by means of rational information—as though sexual problems were *caused* by the ignorance or the irrationality which are actually part of their symptomatology. Ignorance or self-defeating behavior in matters which most people are able to learn from direct experience—and which are now subject to abundant public discussion—is likely to be a symptom of emotional problems quite impervious to rational instruction.

10

living in social systems in which such misperceptions almost unavoidably are imposed by indoctrination, but rather those who live outside such systems.) There must be a need—whether or not we call it pathological—which is gratified by the misperception so obviously in conflict with easily available knowledge. The misperception cannot be corrected unless that need is faced, and the persons experiencing it can gratify it without misperceiving reality.

What has all this to do with social theories and, more specifically, with the widespread hostility to the market which concerns the contributors to this volume? When it comes to social, political or economic ideas, we rarely consider what emotional meaning they have for those who invent or advocate them. Economists, when concerned with social policy, more than others are guilty of continuing a Kantian posture. They unceasingly point out how irrational most of the arguments used against the market are—and they argue brilliantly against the self-defeating attempts of governments to regulate market forces. But they seldom ask why their arguments have so little influence, why the policies they oppose continue, why the ideas they show to be wrong continue their hold on so many people. Ostrichlike, economists tend to ignore the nonrational sources of hostility to the market system.*

*Economists, such as George Stigler, who do ask what causes the success of anti-market forces, try to explain it exclusively

11

If Kant was wrong, so are economists who counter irrational ideologies with rational arguments, who act as though irrational pseudo-reasoning and chiliastic longings can be fought successfully by proper economic reasoning. Union leaders, socialists, academic egalitarians, Marxists, totalitarians and millenarians of every kind have a strong emotional investment in their policies and theories which ultimately leads to ideological and finally to material investment. They cannot be persuaded by any argument, however well it shows that the policy they favor is contrary to the public interest, ineffective or both. The attempt of economists to tutor the emotionally committed is as doomed to failure as the attempts of philosophers to tutor the insane.

Not that economics which deals with the economy on a rational level is not a justifiable enterprise. On the contrary, it is essential: it tells us what the right economic policy or system is or at least what policies or systems cannot achieve our ends. And philosophy too, Kantian or other, helps us understand what we are or should be doing. But neither philosophy nor economics has any therapeutic use.* They cannot of themselves persuade

---

in terms of the rational economic interests of the protagonists. They ignore emotions or treat them as necessarily dependent variables.

*Wittgenstein's "therapeutic" use of philosophy was not "therapeutic" in the psychological sense. It cured wrong reasoning in those whose disturbance was philosophical rather than psychological.

12

anyone to follow correct policies or to learn to reason correctly, unless he is independent enough of emotional predispositions to reason in ways not predetermined by them. Correct economic arguments help only people who have been cured or are on the mend—people capable of rational argument on the subject and responsive to it. Correct arguments do not cure those who reason badly or misperceive when their reasoning or their misperception gratifies a strong social or personal need to believe in something irrational. Nor is economics diagnostic: it cannot tell us wherefrom the need to argue and perceive the world in distorted terms arises.

Since Kant wrote, new sciences have arisen to concern themselves precisely with those things that Kant improperly claimed for philosophy. Psychology explores what motivates people and makes them acquire specific thinking processes and belief systems. The sociology of knowledge (which should be called sociology of belief) explores the situations which cause whole groups of people to share specific beliefs and attitudes. Why, then, have sociologists and psychologists not enlightened us much about the sources of hostility to the market system?

The answer to this paramount question must be suggestive and tentative, rather than conclusive. One cannot disregard the fact that sociologists and psychologists themselves often have had a hostile or at least an ambivalent attitude toward the market system. Surely this is true of Auguste Comte, who named, if he did not father, sociology, and of Emile Durkheim, even though he refused to call himself a socialist (his followers became socialists); Max Weber and Georg Simmel* too, each in a different and ambivalent way, were hostile to the market system. Earlier, Karl Marx, who impregnated most sociological thinking, even if his paternity is not always recognized, candidly raised the banner of hostility to the market or capitalist economy, prophesying as well as advocating its "inevitable" demise. None of these men (not even Marx) were Marxists. Yet each, for reasons of his own, displayed at least ambivalence toward the market system. This may be one of the major reasons why the sources of social hostility to the market system so rarely have become the subject of scholarly investigation and why the disadvantages of the market system, real and fancied, have been magnified so often. It is hard to investigate a hostility one shares, easier to investigate what one is hostile to, so as to rationalize one's hostility rather than to have to analyze it.

What has been said about sociologists can be said about psychologists as well. Freud was not a socialist. He saw that the millenarian hopes of Marxists and socialists were inconsistent with the human psyche, which he had explored. But he did not

*I deliberately neglect exceptions such as Spencer and classical American sociology: they have lost whatever influence they had even in their homelands.

14

understand or care for the free market system. In this respect he was tone deaf (as he was to music). Many of his followers—loyal or schismatic—were socialists or communists: Otto Fenichel, Helene Deutsch, Alfred Adler, Wilhelm Reich, Erich Fromm and many others.*

Since it is easier to explore the ideology of others than one's own, the sources of hostility to the market system have not been explored much so far. The rank and file of intellectuals were and remain hostile in various degrees to the market system and thus reluctant to explore the sources of the hostility they shared and expressed. (Some motivations for their hostility are suggested in the essays which follow.) Yet, who but the intellectuals could possibly explore the source of this hostility?

The papers which follow were commissioned by the Liberty Fund, Inc., to begin this exploration. They were read at a conference held at the Homestead, Hot Springs, West Virginia, in March 1975. Professor Bauer's paper (published here in a revised form) appeared as a chapter in *The First World and The Third World* (edited by Karl Brunner, University of Rochester Policy Center, 1978). My own paper has been published in *The Public Interest,* Fall 1976 (the present version has been revised). The remaining papers and comments, re-

*The whole Frankfurt Institute—Horkheimer, Adorno, not to speak of Marcuse, et al.—labored mightily for a synthesis of psychoanalysis and Marxism.

15

vised by their authors, are published here for the first time.

My own paper explores the vulnerabilities of the market system—the extent to which they are unavoidable, the specific forms they take, and the attacks they invite.

Professor Feuer's paper delves into the motives and personalities of leaders and followers in the attack on the market system, particularly among U.S. intellectuals.

Professor Bauer concerns himself with the transmission of hostility to the market system from Western to undeveloped countries. He discusses how the hostility is carried from the developed to the undeveloped countries, where it develops new virulence. Bauer also suggests the social and psychological reasons which cause the leading strata in the undeveloped countries to become so readily infected.

Professor Rothman's epilogue warns us against confusing the irrationality of sources of hostility to the market system with the rational or irrational justifications of that hostility.

The comments by Messrs. Roger Starr, Dale Vree and Nathan Glazer cast additional, often critical light from different and interesting angles on the subjects elaborated in the papers commented on.

The discussion at the conference was lively, illuminating and remarkably coherent. Perhaps it should have been included in this volume. But an oral witticism, an epigram or argument, may not

16

appear to be as felicitous in print as it was in appropriate context. *Verba volant scripta manent* is both a description and a prescription. Thus, it was decided to offer only the written papers. I hope they will instruct the readers as much as they did the participants at the conference.

Ernest van den Haag

New York City
June 14, 1979

1

Confusion, Envy, Fear and Longing*

Ernest van den Haag

According to Friedrich von Hayek, "it is meaningless to describe the manner in which the market distributes the good things of this world among particular people as just or unjust." He is quite right. Justice is as irrelevant to the functioning of the market, to economic efficiency and to economics, as it is to a computer or to meteorology. But it is not irrelevant to our attitude toward these things. People will tolerate a social or economic system, however efficient, only if they perceive it as just.

Even if everybody were better off in a market system than in any other, people might sufficiently resent the inequality with which the market dis-

*Ernest van den Haag's essay, "Confusion, Envy, Fear and Longing," is a revised version of "Economics Is Not Enough —Notes on the Anticapitalist Spirit" which first appeared in *The Public Interest*, Number 45, Fall 1976. Copyright © 1976 by National Affairs, Inc.

tributes its benefits to become hostile to it. Only if
that inequality could be morally justified would it
appear to be acceptable. Or if, as in former times,
the market were accepted as a divine or natural
creation, an unalterable fact, which "it is meaningless to describe as just or unjust." But we no longer
so regard the market. It has been secularized together with the rest of our institutions. The various
moral justifications available in the past melted
away when the traditional beliefs and customs on
which they rested were eroded by the market
forces themselves and the kind of free, secular society they created. Most important, no new *moral*
justification has replaced the traditional ones: The
market has not been able to come up with a moral
doctrine that justifies it since the decline of the
bourgeois ethos that linked economic reward and
moral virtue. On the contrary, the rational tem-
perament of the market destroys supportive social
mythologies—such as the various natural law doctrines—as an acid may eat away the material
needed to contain and confine it.

The market does provide incentive rewards to
those who produce what it values; but these rewards are seldom felt to be distributed justly from
a moral point of view. Moral justice must indeed
differ from market effects—unless the production
of market value, which constitutes economic
merit, is defined as moral merit. This is what John
Bates Clark did and what Ayn Rand does once
more. Such an identification is convenient and, for
a while, it was supported by tradition. But today

success is as often identified with personal vice as with personal virtue.

Anyway, the identification of moral and economic merit confuses the *de facto* historical (if you please, natural) conditions of legal entitlement to rewards, or of actual appropriation, with the justification thereof: The argument identifies what is to be justified with its moral justification. Robert Nozick does so in a sophisticated way in his *Anarchy, State, and Utopia.* He takes as self-evident the answer to a question he barely asks: "Why is it just that each of us be the exclusive beneficiary of his own legitimate efforts?" It is his natural right, Nozick declares. To which the inevitable response is: But nature never told *me* that. Nor does Nozick explain why, if nature's will is what he says it is, we should follow it when we could do otherwise.

It seems to me that rights (as distinguished from claims) are granted by social authority. It is for us to decide what they should be. Nature merely sets limits to the range of the possible; within it we have to decide. Our decision must depend on justice as we see it, and on efficiency. Even if a particular set of historical conditions were shown to be unavoidable, and to make our decision unavoidable, it would not therefore become just. But history, though never avoided, is never unavoidable.

The morally and the economically justified distribution differ. They must, because economic and moral criteria differ. Whatever independent definitions are chosen, moral desert certainly cannot be identified with economic desert as it is determined by the market. An appealing movie actress, a shrewd promoter, a successful manager, or investor, or advertising man, or inventor or oil discoverer, are not morally superior to a faithful nurse or worker, to a courageous lifesaver or war veteran, to a needy child, a great poet or philosopher. At least, I am not familiar with any ethical theory that holds them to be. Yet the former may earn much more than the latter, and for good enough *economic* reasons: What they offer has more market value. But they do not earn more because they are morally more deserving than those who are less well rewarded. (Interestingly enough, wealthy actresses are rarely resented, while wealthy bankers are—perhaps because the assets of actresses are more visible and appealing than those of bankers. Still, the wealth of neither, actress or banker, is produced or justified by moral superiority.)

INEQUALITY, MORALITY AND EFFICIENCY

Equality of opportunity—i.e., procedural justice— is of little help here. A procedurally just lottery leads to unequal results; so does the most scrupulously fair competition. The results can still be felt to be unjust, although the injustice of the lottery is attributed to "fate," whereas people now believe that the inequality of the results of competition must be attributed to the injustice not of fate but of capitalists and of capitalism. Indeed, equality of opportunity may intensify the resentment generated by the unequal results it necessarily produces, even if people in reasonably similar circumstances compete in the procedurally most fair manner.[1] Ultimately such resentments go back to envy of just those natural gifts and differences, including luck, that equality of opportunity highlights. The differences seem unjust because they do not reflect any felt or accepted *moral* differences.

It is difficult even to morally justify the unequal social results produced by altogether natural gifts. Why should an attractive girl, in addition to enjoying her natural beauty, also be able to use it to become rich? Why should she be more gifted than others in the first place? Why should the person whom nature disabled, in addition to suffering the pain inherent in the disability, also be poor? And can we not say equally well of mental gifts and disabilities what has been said of physical ones? The inclination as well as the ability to make successful efforts is not independent of inborn physical and psychological gifts and of environmental advantages and disadvantages. One must grant then that the moral aversion to the unequal results of the market system, or of any system ideally based on equality of opportunity, has something to commend it besides envy. Indeed the Judaic and Christian ethic of the past proclaimed the injustice of the world, whether that world be characterized by equal or unequal opportunity. The world certainly included the market. But traditional religious ethic did not attribute that injustice to the government, or to an evil economic system; rather it was part of the nature of this world. And religion proclaimed that all unjust inequalities would be compensated for in another world.

Although its distributional inequalities may lack moral justification, the market system is likely to lead to superior economic results for everyone, because the market is so efficient that even if only a small percentage of the national income is redistributed, more is available for redistribution to those disadvantaged by nature or misfortune than in alternative systems. Through competition the market fosters technical innovation far more than any other system and provides for the replacement of obsolete products and modes of production. This, perhaps more than anything else, makes market systems productive. Not least, the market makes an exceptionally wide dispersal of power and prestige possible, as well as very extensive individual independence. Central planning—the only actual alternative available—by contrast, inhibits the introduction of the new and the replacement of the obsolete. This helps account for its relatively low productivity. And it distributes power and prestige more unequally than the market does.

Quite apart from their lower efficiency and the consequent aggravation of the burden of inequality, alternatives to the market, once actualized, are likely to arouse no less hostility than the market does. For any such alternative such as centralized planning runs up against the actual sources of a hostility which in the end may turn out to be directed toward all rational systems of distributing rewards rather than to any specific system of production or distribution.

Popular feeling would surely be as opposed to an unequal distribution according to political deserts as it is now to an unequal distribution according to economic deserts. An equal distribution, were it possible, would surely be rejected too: It would not appropriately reward unequal merits and efforts. We would not be satisfied if the indolent worker were to get as much as the hard worker, the careless fool as much as a careful and intelligent craftsman. Equal treatment of unequals cannot be just, as Aristotle pointed out. Merits differ. Moreover, so do capacities to enjoy things or to feel miserable. Hence equality in the distribution of income is as unsatisfactory to the moral sense as inequality is. We all want *moral* desert to be rewarded. But there is no satisfactory measure of moral deserts; as each of us defines them, moral deserts are incommensurable. No system of equality or inequality will satisfy our sense of justice, for neither rewards our own moral desert as each of us feels it ought to be rewarded.

However, it is precisely because they cannot identify moral and economic value that people wish to link them. It outrages the sense of justice that, in the market, the services of persons perceived as morally less deserving often are valued more than the services of persons perceived as morally more deserving—although the very people outraged by it bring this result about by their willingness to pay more for the economically more valuable services. After all, that is why those who render such services get more, regardless of moral desert. But people also want to change the result they produce to reflect their sense of justice, at least to some degree.

The uneasy and unstable relation between economic and moral valuation exists within people, not merely within social systems. It used to be a function of religion to stabilize this relationship by promising eternal rewards and punishments to offset temporal injustice. But the modern world, as created by capitalism, is secular in its basic modes of thought. It does not take religious faith seriously enough to assuage the moral discomfort capitalism creates.

Yet, if resources are to be allocated to produce the total output valued most highly by allocators (in a free market by consumers), and if production is to be maximized, then inequalities of income, status and power are unavoidable. Work must be rewarded by income, and the income earned by each worker must depend on how much work he does, on his skill, and on the value placed on it. Ability, skill, the inclination and the opportunity to work differ, as does the economic value of the work done and, therefore, the reward. Market value depends on scarcity, on how much is available relative to demand. Scarcities differ; therefore so do the incomes earned for performing services. The socioeconomic structure—the distribution of inequalities—always arises independently of the criteria of moral justice used to judge it.

Rewards must be distributed according to the market value of services for the sake of efficiency, if not justice. Critics who have conflated objections to the market's failure to do moral justice with objections to its efficiency in calling forth production are simply wrong. A look at the alternatives to the market is altogether persuasive; they are less efficient by far. And it is easy to see that the socialist systems instituted to aim directly at moral justice so far have not been notable for achieving any more of it than market systems; and they grant less individual freedom. But such rational knowledge is of little help in dispelling the resentment against the market—or the longing for an ideal system in which a just government justly rewards moral merits.

On closer analysis this longing rests on nonrational fantasies: Each of us secretly hopes that his essential superiority will be recognized in an ideal system. Albeit unconsciously, revolutionaries as well as reformers place this hope on an ideal government, which functions as a true *parens patriae,* a just and omniscient parent—just as a gambler places his hope on Dame Fortuna, who inexplicably but certainly and justly will love him best, and prefer him—as mother should have done.

THE RESENTMENT OF INTELLECTUALS

Intellectuals resent the market because it makes people pay for economic value. Moral value is left out in the cold—and so are intellectuals, who are the producers of moral value, of moral approval and disapproval for public consumption. (Lately, quite a few intellectuals produce moral values that have market value too. But the main contingent of humanists and social scientists, the traditional intellectuals, still feel deprived of the power and income they believe they deserve by virtue of their virtue.) Hence intellectuals long for and have often designed utopias, generated by reason and desire, though bereft of reality or even possibility. They would reward morally valuable activities— their own kind of activities—rather than economic ones. Unfortunately such unworldly and incorruptible designs have fostered the institution of corrupt worldly systems.

In any actual social system, rewards for moral excellence are not likely to be prominent; and they are less likely to be frequent in nonmarket systems than in market systems. If the economic decision mechanisms of the market are abolished, they must be replaced by political (governmental) mechanisms for distribution. Just as the market rewards economic services, political distribution systems will reward political services—i.e., services in the production and distribution of power. Actual distribution will necessarily depend on political power and be as independent of moral desert as it is in the market. We will be stuck with a system of distribution felt to be as morally irrelevant and arbitrary as that of the market, but which certainly will leave us poorer, because it provides stronger incentives for unproductive political activities than for productive economic services.

Further, the government can distribute income independently of a market only by depriving individuals or groups (such as corporations) of the right to produce and sell what they think buyers are willing to pay for. This is indeed what full-fledged socialism does. What is to be produced does not depend on the demands of consumers but on the independent decisions of government planners; production, therefore, is more likely to serve the purposes of planners, of the government, than those of any or of all individual consumers. Citizens, unable to decide for themselves what to produce or sell, would lose one freedom. To keep us bereft of it, the government would eventually have to deprive us of political freedom as well; as the sole producer and employer, the government would find it easy to restrict political freedom; the government will do so, for political freedom could be used to replace central with individual plans. Shorn of institutional defense, individual liberty could not survive long.

However, there is little doubt that alternatives to the market system would increase the relative power and income, if not the freedom, of intellectuals and para-intellectuals—of bureaucrats and of clerks. They would be in charge. The alternative to the market is bureaucracy, whatever label is affixed to it. At present, it can limit the play of market forces. But in a planned economy bureaucracy would replace the market by making decisions concerning allocation and production. In the end the power, income and prestige taken from entrepreneurs would go to bureaucrats.

Many genuine intellectuals—specialists in the invention, development and analysis of ideas—believe that their merits will be recognized so that they will occupy the positions in the bureaucracy that would enable them to benefit from this redistribution and in turn to practice their benevolence on the population at large. Experience suggests otherwise. Major power positions are likely to be taken not by genuine intellectuals, but by specialists in the manipulation of bureaucratic power. They are no more likely to be intellectuals than bureaucrats are now.

THE AUTHORITY OF TRADITION

While capitalist countries live in the greatest prosperity the world has ever seen, the supporters of the market system are an embattled minority, certainly among the intellectuals, but also among other groups. Perennial moral vulnerabilities do not explain why the complaints against the injustice of the market system have such wide appeal now. We must turn to historical changes to account for the decline in the level of approval.

The religious emphasis of the past was on divine sanction for traditional or deserved inequalities. In the world beyond, they would be redistributed according to true moral desert—but also greatly magnified. (What inequality can possibly exceed that between heaven and hell?) Religion did not equate moral with economic merit, but neither did it object to economic rewards for economic merits, holding that moral merit need not be rewarded in this world. Thus, limits were set to envy and to the clamor for equality or moral justice in this world. Moral justice was to come in the next. Religion opposed no particular economic system but, indiscriminately, any emphasis on material advancement. Psychologically (though not logically) this amounted to support for almost any *status quo.*

With the Renaissance and the Reformation, many religious thinkers came to believe that economic success might be a sign of divine approval. To strive for it thus became more legitimate. But when they bent their gaze from the heavens to this earth, men came to expect rewards here and now for their efforts and merits. They became altogether disenchanted with religion, once they no longer regarded the life to come as the goal of life on earth. Demanding to be rewarded justly here and now, men wanted to be rewarded more, and more equally, than they had been. Religion has since picked up the cue: Where it tries to regain influence, the ecclesiastical establishment does so by fanning the widespread hostility to capitalism and inequality by insisting on justice, i.e., equality, in this world and by deemphasizing the next. Churches, as distinguished from fundamentalist sects, now try to gratify the longing for moral justice by advocating inchoate welfare measures

31

rather than by pointing to heaven and emphasizing salvation.

As long as tradition itself could still confer legitimacy, inequality was not seriously questioned even without religious sanction. But the market economy destroys traditional beliefs and attachments; it does not rest on custom; it believes in progress, not piety. The market does not believe it makes sense for anyone to do anything simply because his father or grandfather did it.

Further, the inherent mobility of the market incessantly redistributes inequalities, so that they cannot be legitimized by tradition, which requires continuity. To be sure, alternative systems also lack tradition as a source of legitimacy. But they have defenses which capitalism lacks. They are apprehended as transitional stages to ultimate justice and equality, while the market economy is too rational and has existed too long now to be accepted as a preface to the millennium. So far, the socialist promise has survived nonredemption, just as major religions have survived the postponement of salvation *ad kalendas graecas.*

THE DILEMMA OF POVERTY

If to be poor still meant to have less than what one physically needs to survive, poverty would touch only a few among the poor in the United States (though not elsewhere). However, once biological needs are met for most of the poor, poverty is defined by history and society, and refers not to physical needs nor to the size of incomes, high or low, but to the social judgment passed on income differences. Thus, in the United States, adults whose income is less than half of the average are judged to be poor, regardless of the absolute size of their income. Yet, the traditional notion of poverty, involving hunger, destitution and distress, still shapes our attitude to it, still evokes the horror it always did. After all, that notion was quite realistic for millennia and is still all too real in much of the world.

Because of the dread associated with poverty, we would like to see it abolished. Yet, although many battles have been won, and more can be, the "war against poverty" cannot be won, since poverty has come to mean inequality, not plain misery. Anything but a totally equal distribution of income necessarily puts some people at the top and others at the bottom. Just as the top group will be called rich, the bottom group will be called poor. Howevermuch the size of the bottom group is decreased, or its distance from the others diminished (and that is where battles have been won), the remaining distance will not be perceived as insignificant: Those at the bottom continue to be regarded as poor by themselves and others, just as those at the top continue to be perceived as rich.

Now, contrary to the hopes of reformers (and to the fears of revolutionaries), the lessening of the distance between the poor and others, and the decrease in the number of the poor, have actually added to the resentment of the poor.[2] The smaller and fewer social distances become, the more irksome they seem, for they stand out more. And improvements often generate expectations of further improvements. These expectations tend to grow more rapidly than the improvements do until they finally exceed possibilities. (Indeed, this is a major source of the perennial pressure for the expansion of government expenditures on the poor, and ultimately for the inflation governments find so hard to avoid.)

The habitual is regarded as inevitable and the inevitable is tolerated. But the inadequate, the unfulfilled promise, is always resented. Reduction of inequalities suggests that any specific remaining inequality is not inevitable. Hence, all reductions short of full equality are felt to be incomplete. Wherefore the resentment of the poor has increased; when acknowledged, or justified, it is seldom seen for what it is: the effect of diminished poverty. To see resentment as the effect of improvement seems paradoxical because contrary to our expectations. The paradox which is within ourselves, not in the social reality, is readily explained. When rich and poor were as "two nations," the poor experienced and therefore envied one another more than the rich, who were socially too remote even for envy. No longer isolated by vast and apparently insurmountable distances in education and living conditions, the poor now share much of the common outlook. In particular, they share the consuming ambitions of the non-poor, brought home day in and day out by television.

34

Yet, being poor, they continue to lack the means to fulfill these ambitions, and they resent what they now learn to perceive as "deprivation."

Indeed, the social perception of poverty has changed altogether. No one, rich or poor, believes any longer that poverty is part of a divinely sanctioned, efficient or even tolerable social order—let alone the individual responsibility or fault of the poor. More than merely a sign of systemic inefficiency, poverty is seen now as an injustice, an unmet responsibility of the rich, who are felt to be guilty of depriving the poor. (This notion now prevails among, as well as within, nations.) No longer accepted as part of the *physiology* of the body social, poverty has come to be treated as social *pathology.* Yet, it has been so redefined as to become as unavoidable as inequality is. The pathology created by definition is usually regarded as inherent not in the definition but in the private ownership of capital, which is thought to cause exploitation and deprivation. Thus, the poverty of the poor is blamed on the wealth of the rich and on the market system that makes both possible.

The poor themselves as long as they were a majority, or at least a plurality, accepted their condition as natural. So did everybody else. But the poor have become a minority, and rather than separate and different, they feel isolated and passed by. Thus, rich and poor feel uncomfortable with the market, or "capitalism," even though, or because, it distributes the good things of life far less unequally than any other system ever did; even

35

though, or because, it produces far more of them. Wealth now produces guilt feelings as often as comfort. The rich seldom feel that their wealth is deserved; their children almost never do. The approval of inequality by God, nature and society has been withdrawn. The market system stands naked to its enemies, exceedingly vulnerable to the interaction between resentments and guilt feelings.

While some things can be done to assuage guilt feelings—albeit with questionable success—very little can be done to reduce resentment. Redistributions short of total equality are not likely to reduce it. Nor would poverty disappear if the "needs" of the poor were met by making "essentials" available to all, regardless of ability or effort. For, unlike survival minima, "needs" are not biologically given; they are socially generated desires. As more things become available through higher incomes, more things are felt to be essential to meet the needs created by the availability of these things. Biologically dispensable things become "essentials" when they are perceived as essential —whether they be new kinds of food, housing, cigarettes, legal and medical services, recreation or plumbing. As Shakespeare realized long before 96 percent of families on welfare in New York had television sets, ". . . our basest beggars/ Are in the poorest things superfluous." The poor feel no fewer needs now than people who earn average incomes. Hence, their needs cannot be met while they are poor—i.e., as long as they have less than average incomes.

Further, as welfare payments make the poverty of the unemployed or unemployable poor less depriving and punishing, some otherwise employable poor people become unable or unwilling to take employment at market rates. Employability is easily reduced, without fakery, by child bearing, drug addiction, sickness or selectivity with respect to jobs. One is unconsciously likely to make oneself unemployable when the price paid for unemployability makes it attractive. Once poverty becomes a marketable service, its supply rises as the price it brings does, relative to other services, such as work. Thus, either welfare grants must be kept within narrow limits so that the poor live quite differently from the non-poor and the production of marketable poverty becomes unattractive to those capable of work (of producing other marketable services)—or reduced employability (increased marketable poverty) must be accepted. We seem to feel too guilty to do the first while the second leads into the quagmire in which we now find ourselves: less poverty, associated with increased relief rolls. Whatever can be said morally for present welfare payments, they are self-defeating not only economically but also psychologically. Recipients feel no less poor, nor less resentful than they would without subsidies, and their number tends to increase as we buy the poverty that they produce, and thereby create a demand for it. In turn, guilt feelings increase as the number of welfare recipients does.

The resentments of the disadvantaged ultimately are directed against the market system, which generates inequality. Actually, so does any other system. But the market becomes the target for those living in it, while distant systems are idealized. The utopian grass of remote societies, or fantasies, always grows greener.[3]

God once willed apparent injustice, and faith justified it. He was "justly secret—and secretly just" (St. Augustine). Without Him only the social system is left to blame. And no system can survive in the end if it is perceived as unjust by those who feel disadvantaged in it and by those who benefit from it.

CHILDREN AND SOCIALISM

Why are the young now so much more hostile to the market than the young were in the past? Up to the 20th century in the upper classes children were thought of as heirs. Raised to preserve and secure the status and fortune of the family, they were trained, educated and, above all, disciplined accordingly. Ambitions and expectations were directed to the assumption of their role. Deviations were regarded with horror. Nineteenth-century novels, French, German or English, amply illustrate this, as does Verdi's *La Traviata,* based on Dumas' *La Dame aux Camélias.*

Before the 19th century, family status, secured legally, was somewhat less dependent on the incumbent's conduct and, therefore, on his training. By the 19th century the aristocratic estate system was replaced by the bourgeois class system. Training and education became essential if status was to be preserved. Upper-class parents, particularly fathers, had the disciplinary means to impose education and to define the role of their children, because the child's own status, income and future career depended almost entirely on the fortune and the connections of his parents. The threat of disinheritance was quite effective in keeping children in line.

In the upper classes children were thought of as investment goods. Fathers were able to ensure a proper return on pain of disinheritance. In the lower classes children also were treated as investment goods, but in a different way: They were current revenue producers, and they provided social security in old age. In both classes, then, parents had a strong interest in regulating the conduct of their offspring—and the power to do so.

This situation has radically changed. Children are no longer expected to preserve, secure or produce anything for their parents. They have become consumption goods, to be enjoyed for their own sake, like pets. Wherefore, they are treated like pets: No serious demands are made of them. Parents want to be loved more than respected or obeyed; they leave the children free to "find themselves" rather than transmit external social demands to them. No expectations are entertained that children will continue family fortunes or have their conduct regulated by the parental will once they reach the age of reason. Anyway, the disciplinary means available to parents have become extremely weak. The threat of disinheritance is nearly meaningless; taxes greatly diminish what can be left; and children have the ability to earn reasonable incomes independently. Only one family in a thousand derives any significant income from inheritance now. (The proportion of families benefiting from inheritance may not have been greater in the past. But in the past these were the only wealthy families.) With very few exceptions the advancement, status and economic success of the child in an affluent capitalist society do not—or, at least, need not—depend any longer on parental inheritance or connections.

As parental power declined, parental authority became a problem for children (and for sociologists). It was to be rebelled against in any way available. The rebellion has succeeded fairly well, and the ability of the older generations to transmit the culture and the discipline of the past has been weakened. But many young people who find it no longer satisfying to rebel against parental authority—it is no fun to fight what has become pudding —rebel against reality itself (e.g., by drug addiction) or, at least, against social discipline. The market is demonstrably less than just: what better target for hostility? Thus, the young, if they do not want to destroy the market altogether, want to do good, to make amends for its injustices. They are not taught that producing what people value—as demonstrated by their willingness to pay for it—is to do good. They perceive production for the market as evil, for the motive is not altruistic, and the effects are tainted by the motive.

In all major social systems the motivation for work is to extend one's control over goods and services. This motivation—called greed or acquisitiveness when disliked—does not appear to be more widespread or intensive in a market system than in any other developed economy. Thus, socialist economies, as do capitalist ones, reward performance—political more than economic performance, however—with income, power and prestige. Promotion under socialism, as it does under capitalism, means more of these. There is no reason to think that the motives of people in the Soviet Union are different from their motives in the United States. But a socialist economy may have a psychological advantage. Increases in income and promotion in status are, as it were, officially regarded as morally deserved—just as promotion from assistant to associate professor at Harvard is. This relieves acquisitiveness and ambition of the selfish aura that bothers us.

In the market, high incomes are achieved rather than bestowed from above. One achieves them by performing the services that are demanded. But there is no blessing by authority, no sanction that tells us we deserve what we get. Indeed, we have always been somewhat ambivalent toward our own greed. Perhaps we can't stand it in the naked, unadorned form that confronts us in the market economy—without the blessing of authority that absolves us of guilt. "It is not from the benevolence of the butcher, the brewer or baker that we expect our dinner, but from their regard to their own interest," Adam Smith wrote. Reliance on "their own interest" makes the market work so well. It is also what makes the children as hostile to capitalist society as they are to "selfishness."

Socialism has still another psychological advantage. It offers a visible hand in the form of central planning, instead of the invisible one of the market. The psychological advantage of visibility is great: It reassures people. In contrast to planning, the market is automated. Unlike the visible, manual controls of planners, automatic mechanisms—whether markets or a natural order functioning by itself, not planned and presided over by a God—seem morally unintelligible and psychologically desolate, precisely because it is "meaningless to describe [them] as just or unjust."

Besides not gratifying our anthropomorphic expectations, the absence of a visible and tangible directive authority, when confused with an absence of direction, as it usually is, also leads to the accusation that the market exemplifies "anarchy of production." Yet the "invisible hand" of profit and loss directs the market to respond to consumer demands and coordinates production far more sensitively than any central planning authority would be able to do—if it wanted to. It does not; the point of planning is to impose the official planner's plans, by defeating the plans of consumers when inconsistent with his. Yet, multiple individual plans *automatically* coordinated are simply not perceived as "planning," whereas a central plan is. Individuals, each pursuing his own plan, form a crowd on Fifth Avenue; they are not perceived as forming a planned, organized whole; a centrally directed military parade is.

EX ORIENTE LUX?

Nearly a hundred years ago August Bebel said that "anti-Semitism is the socialism of the middle class." It was a correct insight into the psychological function of both ideologies. However, there is a reversal now: For the intellectuals at least, socialism takes the place of anti-Semitism. As anti-Semitism once told the middle class, socialism now tells the intellectuals where evil comes from and how it must be abolished. As the "anti-Semitism" of the intellectuals, hostility to the market is likely to be as impervious to rational information as ideologies that gratify emotional needs usually are. It is only from experience that people may learn that the abolition of markets will actually intensify their grievances. Perhaps the communist segment of the world will provide the educational experience needed to keep the free market elsewhere. However, the glorification of the late Mao's China by the intellectuals suggests how hard it is for any reality to disabuse them.

43

FOOTNOTES

1. It does not always, as the attitude of sports fans testifies. Psychological exploration of the feelings generated by equality of opportunity and unequal results is urgently needed. Meanwhile, while lip service is paid to equality of opportunity, objections to the unequal results produced are usually rationalized by suggesting that the unequal results *ipso facto* prove that opportunity was not equal.

2. Cf. Freud's "Narcissism of Small Differences," or Tocqueville's many references to this experience. Note also that if income differences were to be wiped out, other more fundamental differences would loom large and would be resented instead.

3. Goethe's Mephisto was naïve in saying that "all theory is gray and green life's golden tree." Fantasy (whether or not called theory) can be greener than life, for it can be colored by desire alone.

2

A Comment on "Confusion, Envy, Fear and Longing"

Roger Starr

Ernest van den Haag very eloquently, I think, examines some of the reasons why our contemporaries insist on turning their backs on a form of productive organization which depends on private ownership, in general, of the means of production. He has sought to explain why they expect more from a type of productive organization in which the means of production are owned by government and operated under the commands of a hierarchical bureaucracy.

In my terms, Dr. van den Haag must be considered an optimist. I say this not because I share the belief of the people he describes. Most emphatically, I share Dr. van den Haag's doubt that better things will come from public ownership and a shift away from market determinations of the quantity and type of goods produced. I believe that *worse* things follow such a shift. Sometime I should like to explore the significance of the metaphor I have used almost unconsciously to define a more humane state of affairs; I have, you will note, used the expression "better *things*" to describe an improvement generally in the human condition.

I call Dr. van den Haag an optimist because he suggests that however misguided they may be, the sentiments that arouse hostility to the free market are in a sense rational. These sentiments spring, as he puts it, from confusion, envy, fear and longing. Since all four of these sentiments are destructive, the effort to cure them is a rational effort. Dr. van den Haag seems to believe that men and women have the means to effectuate a cure. Dr. van den Haag tells us that envy on the part of the poor of the nearby affluence of the rich produces impatience with the market mechanism and private ownership. It might be possible to eradicate envy, at least for a period of time, by diversion, entertainment, hyperpatriotism, bear-baiting. Dr. van den Haag also tells us that the intelligentsia flees from the free market ideology because it cannot equate market distribution with a sense of abstract justice and then finds that its own ambition for power can be expressed in a socially acceptable way by urging that it will lead a bureaucracy which will substitute its own perceived justice for the random injustices of the marketplace. The urge to redress market injustice seems to me a rational impulse that might be dealt with; we might load the members of the intelligentsia with honors and money to persuade them to keep their hands, or more important, their brains off the market and the injustices they find in it. But in my gloomier moments, of which this is one, I would disagree with the view I impute to Dr. van den Haag, that opposition to the free market is based on a rational desire for justice or power. I would argue that opposition to the marketplace and to the private ownership of the means of production is founded on a deeper impulse which is much more difficult to contend with.

I suggest that the root of much—perhaps not all, but much—of the hostility to free markets comes from man's difficulty in dealing with the most human of activities, the making of conscious choices. I assume that while there is a tremendous human yearning for the power to make choices— and this is a power which the investment of human effort in capital has demonstrably increased among men—there is at the same time a correspondingly great fear that one will be stuck with the consequences of one's choices. The possibility of making a choice between different kinds of bread suggests the wide distribution of a power almost unheard of outside kings' palaces two hundred years ago and imbues ordinary men and women of the capitalistic era with a sense of power. Nonetheless, the *act* of choosing, of picking, if you will, a rye bread over a pumpernickel, a sliced white loaf over an unsliced Italian loaf with sesame seeds, immediately deprives one of the power of choice. The choice has been made and one must exist with its consequences. One must accept the fact that one may be wrong and that in a very real sense, particularly in more important matters—such as selecting the location of a home or the furniture one shall live with, or a career, or a set of values for one's life, or the form of political organization which one will choose as most tolerable among alternatives—the making of a choice is truly irrevocable.

I suggest that in the long sweep of history, the power to make choices day after day, hour after hour, has been confined to a very few people who possessed power in each culture. Most human activity has been confined to such a small compass of competing possibilities that it has not been necessary for ordinary people to make a conscious choice among them. I suggest that the natural urge among men and women for power over their environment, as a protection for themselves against the imminent dangers of life, has led to the proliferation of goods, food, shelter, clothing— and, spectacularly in the last two centuries, this proliferation has given us a giddying power to make conscious choice in the marketplace among alternatives.

EVASION OF CHOICE

To recognize that the *evasion* of choice is a major human activity, one merely has to look at the devices ordinary people have found for evading either the consequences of choice or the pangs of uncertainty that surround the conscious act of choice itself. The simplest form of evasion is assembling sufficient money so that parting with it, in exchange for goods or services, seems so insignificant that the pains of choice are, in effect, limited. Incidentally, to remain poor, perhaps with conscious or unconscious deliberation, is also to evade the necessity of making choices and imposing on oneself the disturbing alternation between sensing power and giving it up which the preparation for choice and the exercise of it provide.

But we are pained witnesses also to the abdication of choice to addiction or psychological compulsion. The addict—whether to alcohol, tobacco, narcotics, food or sex—abandons the process of weighing alternatives and chooses instead to relish the abandonment of his power in a fleeting satisfaction of obsessive hunger. He positively enjoys the loss of power that occurs the moment after one has used it, the extreme distortion of the process of choice which occurs in compulsive gambling; some observers claim to find a desire to lose, the search for punishment that expiates the sin of discarding the power of choice. The responsibility for having chosen wisely or foolishly, the difficulty of accepting the consequences of one's own act, the ease with which one blames outside forces, such as luck, discrimination, injustice, for having chosen wrongly, all seem to indicate that there is a tremendous yearning to avoid having to make choices, so that the evasion of a free market with its plethora of choices constitutes a natural response to the risks of full humanity.

Viewed from the other side, the discovery in the absence of a free market that one has the human power to make choices inspires a level of courage that must awe the observer. I am thinking of the extraordinary courage and humanity which characterizes those Russians who discovered the possibility of an alternative choice in the very narrow marketplace of ideas which exists in the Russian socialist state. The gravity, courage and dignity of the Russian opposition, qualities which have been released by the act of choosing not to accept what had been described in iron terms by the state apparatus as the only just way to organize a society, raise our hopes for the human condition to an unprecedented level. As Hilton Kramer, the distinguished art editor of *The New York Times*, has pointed out, the growth of a Russian opposition on the basis of freely exercised choice has produced a new kind of person on the earth, free in a sense which we had forgotten is possible. Those who seek to avoid the responsibilities of individual choice by assigning them to others are missing the essence of what it means to be human.

If I may add a few personal observations on this matter, I should like to talk about the daily spectacle that unfolds in New York City as a result of the abdication of choice in the distribution of a commodity in which the free market has been almost completely supplanted. I am referring, of course, to the market for shelter and the result of the constraints imposed upon that market by the imposition of price controls. Those controls, inci-

50

dentally, have lasted from 1943 to the present time and have recently been extended by the New York City Council at least until 1979. This 36-year stretch is far longer than the existence of the Parisian rent controls in the period between the two wars. My interest in rent controls is not merely in the physical deterioration of structure which inevitably follows the disinvestment by owners and lenders when a species of capital goods is removed from the market for the determination of its price.

My interest in rent control focuses on two aspects of the matter less commonly considered. First is the effect of rent control on public discourse, particularly in the discussion of public officials; I find, though I will not discuss the matter further here, that the persistence of rent control in the face of almost universal private perception by the elected officials that its effects are very different from those which they describe publicly, debases the currency of public opinion and adversely affects the whole legislative process. If one wanted to argue metaphorically, one might say that the disappearance of a free market in any important commodity which is not a natural monopoly must be accompanied by the disappearance of a free market in the ideas concerning that commodity.

Equally interesting, and less commonly remarked on, is the effect of rent control on those who are its intended beneficiaries, those who live in the rent-controlled apartments. The structure of New York's rent control law is such that the current resident of a rent-controlled apartment is shielded against rent increases of more than 7½ percent per year, in any year, for any reason or combination of reasons. This does not mean that the occupant necessarily faces a 7½ percent rise each year; the figure is a maximum, not a minimum; rents may indeed be reduced for cause. But the effect of the imposition of this ceiling on rents is to vitiate the willingness of the tenant to exercise choice about where he or she is to live. Because the tenant enjoys the unique advantage of protected tenure as long as he or she stays in possession, all such tenants say that they "cannot afford to move." They say this even when they are grossly under-occupying the apartment and even when the entire neighborhood around them is caving in from the accumulated neglect of years of under-maintenance. Charles Abrams, the late expert on housing economics, who served as State Rent Control Commissioner in the early 1950s, used to defend his agency's policies on the grounds that they were encouraging the middle class to stay in the city. What, in fact, his policies were accomplishing was the undermining of middle-class responsibility by enabling, indeed forcing, the members of that class to ignore their own personal responsibility for individual rational knowledge. Knowing that the buildings in which they were living were being under-maintained and knowing that they were, in many cases, occupying an unreasonable amount of space, they were nevertheless excused from making the choice about moving or paying a higher rent because *force majeur,* the enacted law, made their own choices for them.

Ultimately, of course, many of these neighborhoods have decayed to the point at which staying becomes positively dangerous; instead of keeping the middle class in the city, even a somewhat demoralized middle class, the effect of rent control has been to stimulate and accelerate the deterioration beyond repair of entire sections of the city in which middle-class families had been living, and, in my view even worse, it has absolved these residents of any personal responsibility for the damage.

LEADERSHIP IN MASS SOCIETY

Perhaps it is difficult to reconcile my description of the flight from choice with the drive, which we all recognize, for power and control. Theoretically opposed to each other, these two impulses are nevertheless quite consistent. In a mass society, local kinship groups and voluntary associations have been stripped of a large measure of their importance. Their leaders have been undercut as figures of authority capable of inspiring the exercise of choice and of establishing the example of personal responsibility. Instead of concentrating on nearby leaders, men and women have come to associate power with large-scale national and ideological movements. As Dr. van den Haag points out, these movements convey the appearance of power through inflation of the currency. The debasement of currency through inflation makes choice more difficult, not less so, because it distorts the monetary standard of comparison which people have customarily used to measure the desirability of alternatives. In a mass society, the price of a mistake is all too often fatal to a molecular individual, unsupported by ties of kinship or affiliation.

Thus, the reasons for labeling myself as gloomier than Dr. van den Haag will I think be obvious. Dr. van den Haag seems to hope that some triumph of rationality will enable men to perceive that the material goals they seek will be provided more effectively in a market economy than one dominated by government bureaucracies which, as he puts it, "plan," rather than discover what people want by their market behavior. I feel that man is not essentially rational, nor entirely dominated by his materialistic impulses or demands. In my view, the deferral of choice comprises a major objective of those who seek to evade the realities of the marketplace. For me, the hope of return to the freedom of the marketplace will be found only after society has had its fill of the narrowed horizons of individual responsibility which the planned and government-owned economy imposes not merely on the production of goods, but on the products of the mind and the imagination. For me, the hope of future acceptance of the responsibility of choice lies on the far side of the experience of the Russian state, exemplified for us by the emergence of these startling, almost religious figures who have come from the darkness of the Soviet world to express human responsibility on a scale we have not seen in many centuries. Their company is surely uncomfortable; they are, if anything, too strong for us to accept as easy companions, but they are, I think, *the* harbingers of that return from anti-freedom, if you will, which we await. The appalling and depressing aspect of their appearance is the reminder of the suffering and terror we shall have to pass through before we are prepared to recapture the responsibilities of our common humanity.

3

Hostility to the Market in Less-Developed Countries*

Peter Bauer

Virulent hostility to the market, as a system and as an outcome of voluntary transactions, dominates the literature on the position of less-developed countries[1] and on the domestic and international policies appropriate for their material progress. The sources of this hostility bear examination.

The validity of arguments can be assessed conclusively on the basis of evidence and logic. The motives or reasons that lead people to accept arguments, hold ideas, or adopt certain stances cannot be established so firmly; their examination, therefore, must involve some conjecture. This does not detract from the importance of the subject. In-

*Peter Bauer's essay, "Hostility to the Market in Less-Developed Countries," has also been published by permission of The Heritage Foundation in *The First World and the Third World,* edited by Karl Brunner (University of Rochester Policy Center Publications).

deed, because ideas have consequences (in Richard Weaver's words) their provenance is a matter of real interest. Nor is one explanation as good as another. Even when formal testing is not possible, observation and analysis can establish significant connections.

Location of sources of hostility to the market presents a special problem, or at any rate, a problem especially pronounced in our context. The activities of Western politicians and intellectuals and of staff members and spokesmen of the official international organizations are a principal factor behind hostility to the market in less-developed countries.[2] Further, some of the most influential exponents of this hostility in the Third World are Westernized or Western-educated people. Thus, much of the hostility to the market that *emanates* from the Third World *originates* in the West.

A qualification may be appropriate here. In emphasizing the Western sources and the role of the international organizations in hostility to the market in the Third World, I do not suggest that spiritual and material attainment there depends on the West. What I do mean is that, in the generation and maintenance of hostility to the market, the role of the West and of individuals, groups, and organizations supported by the West has been highly significant and possibly decisive.

WESTERN ORIGIN OF THIRD WORLD HOSTILITY

Expert Advice

Some passages from prominent academics will illustrate the Western origin of hostility to the market in less-developed countries and the close links between this Western origin and its local expression. Professor Gunnar Myrdal, a Nobel Laureate, is a prominent advocate of the necessity for development of comprehensive planning and socialism. After noting in a much-quoted publication that Third World governments now accept and adopt such policies as indispensable for emergence from poverty and misery, he adds that, "Positive and urgent advice to do so is given to them by all scholars and statesmen in the advanced countries."[3] Elsewhere he writes, "The special advisers to underdeveloped countries who have taken the time and trouble to acquaint themselves with the problem, no matter who they are,. . . . all recommend central planning as the first condition of progress."[4]

The merits of central planning for development are not the key issue in the present context. I am concerned with the contention that governments and experts in advanced countries are unanimous in advising governments of less-developed countries to pursue these policies. Indeed, many economists—and some of the most vocal, articulate, and influential groups with close contacts with governments, international organizations, the press, and large foundations—express these views and endorse these policies. More to the point, only those who support central planning are classed as experts by the media and these institutions. Although prominent academic economists insist that comprehensive planning is demonstrably unnecessary for economic development and is much more likely to retard than to promote it, by Professor Myrdal's definition, they cannot be experts whatever their technical qualifications, academic position, or field of study.

The acceptance of Myrdal's definition is confirmed by Professor John P. Lewis of Princeton University, former Director of the U.S. Agency for International Development in India:

> It has been decided in India that it is the duty of government—and it cannot be delegated—to create and maintain that "growth perspective" which, Albert Hirschman has rightly insisted, is the one *sine qua non* for successful economic development.
>
> Outside supporters of the Indian development process who refuse to accept this proposition well-nigh disqualify themselves from the outset.[5]

Consider also the concluding paragraph of Professor Jagdish Bhagwati's book, *The Economics of Underdeveloped Countries:*

> Indeed, for the idealists among us, the challenge of development represents today the kind of in-

vigorating stimulus for sustained action that the Soviet revolution was for progressive opinion after continual, even though halting, transition to an international framework favorable to rapid economic growth in the underdeveloped world.[6]

Since the Second World War, the effectiveness of the thrust for economic controls in the Third World has been enhanced by the preponderance of opponents of the market in contacts between the West and the Third World, especially in the international transmission of information. What the Third World learns from the West, or about it or about present and past economic relations between the West and Third World countries, comes from or is filtered through opponents of the market. They dominate international reporting, the wire services, documentary films, and entertainment. The academic contacts between the West and the Third World are also dominated by opponents of the market. This influence has been paramount in augmenting the financial and intellectual resources and in enhancing the prestige and effectiveness of Third World opponents of the market. The latter have a virtual monopoly in the local commissions and delegations of the United Nations and its specialized agencies and affiliations; in the research institutions financed by these organizations; in the local operations of the large Western foundations; in international academic exchanges; in the planning teams supplied to Third World governments by American and British universities.

The views of market supporters are so strange to Third World audiences that they sound eccentric, paradoxical, or bizarre, even when voiced by prominent persons, whether foreign or local, but especially when advanced by foreign academics. This is so even when what market supporters say is both simple and obvious. Visiting academics address a public soaked in anti-market ideas, derived from practically all Western visitors and the textbooks and other economic literature reaching these countries. What market supporters say is inconsistent with the material interests and the political and emotional inclinations of local academics, politicians, and civil servants. It is in conflict also with the opinions expressed or endorsed by the resident representatives of the international organizations and the Western foundations and governments, that is, by all major sources of money and patronage.[7] This situation puts great pressure on those local academics and businessmen who are pro-market. Whatever their actual views, they have to operate in societies with a strong authoritarian tradition, where their professional and financial survival depends on the state or on Western academic, intellectual, or financial support. Thus, a market-oriented visitor has little chance of making a lasting impact on public opinion. Nonetheless, the visitor can help market-oriented local academics and businessmen to maintain their bearings, sanity, and self-respect.

An example will illustrate the situation. In 1970 I lectured at about a dozen of the leading Indian universities and economic research institutions. Everywhere it was taken for granted that socialist planning is indispensable for raising the standard of living. According to my various hosts (who, I may add, treated me with impeccable courtesy), the only choice was between what they called Chinese and Soviet models of development. The preponderance of opponents of the market in academic contacts between the West and the Third World has promoted not only the notion that comprehensive central planning or a socialist economy are indispensable for development, but also the idea that such policies promote or even imply social and economic equality; and that they command the overwhelming or even unanimous support of respected academics.[8] The opponents of the market have also travestied the history of prerevolutionary Russia, and the subsequent history and present conditions in the Soviet Union. They also consistently transmit to the Third World those theoretical developments of contemporary economic analysis which emphasize imperfections of the market system. Unfortunately, they never examine the costs and consequences of alternatives to the market system, alternatives which are always presented in idealized form.

The Legacy of Colonialism

Throughout most of its history, British colonial rule was, on the whole, one of limited government —paternalistic and authoritarian, yet limited. But in the closing years of British colonialism, extensive and pervasive government economic controls came to be introduced throughout Africa and to a lesser extent elsewhere.[9] As a result, the ready-made framework of a *dirigiste* or even totalitarian state was handed over by the British to the incoming independent governments.

Many Third World governments would presumably have attempted to establish such institutions and introduce such policies even without colonial rule or, for that matter, foreign aid. But they could hardly have succeeded in organizing or administering them without the examples set by colonial governments or the personnel and money provided by external aid.

The establishment of tightly controlled economies, such as those handed over by the departing British colonial administrators and supported wherever possible by Western aid, reflected the operation of political, intellectual, administrative, and commercial interests and pressures and the vagaries of fashion and convenience. Some of these controls, especially the export monopolies, have served as power bases for Third World politicians who became influential figures on the world scene.

Yet, such policies were not the necessary corollaries of colonialism. In British Africa until the late 1920s and in Southeast Asia until much later, British colonial administrators appreciated the role of the markets and the functions of traders.[10] Official hostility came about largely as a result of an increase in the number of administrators and technicians, who were removed from the realities of economic life and found controls to be tidier than market forces; the growth of intellectual fashions and ideologies hostile to private trading; belief in the efficacy of closely controlled economies, allegedly in the interests of the population but in practice for the political, personal, and financial benefit of politicians and administrators and in some instances for the benefit of influential trading interests. Thus, the livelihood of the great majority of the local population came to depend on governments, often endowed with quasi-totalitarian powers by policies in the closing years of British colonialism.

GROUPS HOSTILE TO THE MARKET

Third World Groups

In less-developed countries, hostility to the market is widespread among the most articulate, influential, and politically effective groups. Replacement of the market by government-imposed economic controls suits the political, emotional, and financial interests of these groups. Among the rural population, the overwhelming majority of the population in most undeveloped countries, there is little sustained hostility to the market. People at large evince little interest in political or public affairs beyond the tribal or village level; throughout the Third World the discrepancy in political effectiveness and in the ability to shape discussion between the urban population and the rural population, and between the vocal and articulate groups and the unorganized, inarticulate groups is very wide —far wider than in the West. We need, therefore, to focus on opinion- and policymakers—largely intellectuals and academics, writers, and media men; literature politicians and administrators, primarily civil servants and to a lesser extent other professional men; and urban businessmen. In some countries, religious leaders and priests are also important agents in our context. (Army officers often play a part in shaping the course of events, but they rarely serve as sources of general ideas.)

The intellectuals, politicians, and administrators are often closely associated. The relative importance of these groups as agents of hostility to the market is to some extent a matter of judgment and is partly arbitrary because the categories so often overlap. On the whole, intellectuals and civil servants, including the staffs and spokesmen of the international organizations, are more important than politicians, army officers, and businessmen. (In some regions, especially Latin America, the priesthood may be an intermediate category.) The latter groups have fewer international contacts and less interest in general issues. They are often ready to acquiesce in hostility to the market and may benefit from it; they are less able, however, to generate it systematically over a wide area of public concern. The close connection between intellectuals—especially academics—civil servants, and politicians, is particularly significant in India.

The great distance of these groups from the rest of the population promotes a feeling of superiority, which suggests to them that they have a right, often rationalized as a duty, to control the economic conduct and the pattern of consumption of their fellowmen. They favor the replacement of the market by state controls. Moreover, planned and socialized economies create positions of power and status for intellectuals, such as do not exist in a market system. Their ideas are also shared by the corresponding groups in the West, but they are much stronger in the Third World, where they can be translated into practice much more easily because of the discrepancy in political effectiveness.

This difference in political effectiveness is magnified by other factors. One of these is the more authoritarian character of the cultures of the Third World; the subjection of the individual to the authority both of rulers and of custom is more extensive and more unquestioned than in the West. Some effects of the authoritarian tradition were reinforced by the attitude of colonial civil servants, who tended to be hostile to the market and to its most active representatives. Civil servants frequently mistrusted traders, whose activities they found unintelligible and who were less susceptible than their subordinates to orders and commands.

International Organizations

The patently insubstantial idea that international trade damages the less-developed world has been generated and propagated by the staffs and associates of the international agencies, especially by the United Nations Secretariat and the Economic Commission of Latin America. These institutions have also assiduously alleged inadequacies of the market system and the consequent necessity of central planning for the development of poor countries. They have consistently favored Third World governments that try to establish state-controlled economies, and they have also often supplied to these governments the personnel for running state export monopolies, state trading companies, and state-run cooperatives, planning commissions, and so forth.

The UN and its affiliates have fostered hostility to the market in more significant ways. They have sponsored and promoted the concept of a broadly uniform less-developed world, or Third World, with substantially identical interests that conflict with those of the Western market economies. Many of the most influential, energetic, and purposeful staff members of the international organizations think of themselves as agents of such a Third World. These organizations have been the major, perhaps the dominant, factor in promoting the concept of the Third World as a united and loving brotherhood of countries exploited by the West.

The international organizations also systematically attempt to unite less-developed countries into a bloc in opposition to representatives of the market economy. They organize informal meetings of representatives of less-developed countries and present briefs for their spokesmen, almost always with an anti-Western thrust. For instance, such a series of meetings was organized by the regional commissions of the United Nations prior to the first United Nations Conference on Trade and Development (1964) to provide Third World countries with briefs (and, incidentally, also to unite them against the West).

Other Groups

There are many people in the West, including some influential groups, who have for various reasons come to dislike or even to hate their own society and some of its institutions, and especially the market system. They seem to be engaged in a civil conflict in which they regard the less-developed countries as allies. They see these countries as a homogeneous and largely united category whose governments and representatives can be relied on to assail both the West and the market system.[11]

Anthropologists and missionaries also constitute sources of hostility to the market in the Third World. They are apt to deplore the disruption of established ways. It is true that the impact of rapid and uneven change can set up severe strains and inflict hardship. But these types of strain or hardship require far more difficult decisions and choices than the imposition of monopolies or other economic controls.

In Western countries, missionaries and churches have become a vocal and articulate source of hostility to the market, chiefly by emphatic allegations of Western guilt for the poverty of the Third World. Such allegations may promote official foreign aid and also the liquidation of Western influence in the Third World—other than that of the international organizations, the churches, and professional humanitarians. These activities of the churches may reflect a desire to be in the swim, to show that they are "relevant." Perhaps more important, the churches now plainly seek a new role for themselves, namely, that of social welfare agencies on behalf of distant peoples. Such sentiments may also be behind their uncritical acceptance of ideas of exploitation.

IDEAS HOSTILE TO THE MARKET

Marxism-Leninism

The sense of superiority of the Westernized and partly Westernized groups in the Third World is often accompanied by a sense of isolation, which is a source of unhappiness. The intellectuals, while

70

feeling much superior to their fellowmen, insist that they represent their societies. They often wish that it were so but know that it is in fact not true.[12] Their sense of isolation compounds the strains arising from the erosion of traditional beliefs and values and from conflicts of loyalties brought about by the impact of comparatively recent contacts with radically different and materially more advanced societies. These situations predispose the intellectuals and the educated classes to an all-embracing creed, especially one that promises emotional integration or reintegration with their fellowmen. Here is a major attraction of Marxism-Leninism.[13] It is imperative to remember the threefold character of Marxism-Leninism: first, it is an intellectual structure of method, analysis, and observation that claims to explain the operation and prospects of society; second, it is also an all-embracing messianic creed promising salvation on earth, at least in the indefinite future—salvation here, if not now; third, it is a program for political action.

The appeal of Marxism-Leninism in the Third World is unrelated either to its merits or defects as an intellectual structure. It derives from the all-embracing messianic creed and from the political program, from the promise of salvation on earth, and from the promise of a society in which the rulers enjoy enormous power over their fellowmen while they are simultaneously emotionally integrated with them. The appeal is reinforced by the Marxist doctrine of exploitation, the idea that poverty is always the result of an exploitative social system; the presence of an intellectual structure, which, however defective, confers intellectual respectability on a messianic creed; and the political and military successes of Communist parties and movements that have seized control of two of the largest and most powerful countries in the world. The socialist influence in the media and over the transmission lines ensures that the most is made of these successes and also that the social and economic costs of the domestic policies are understated or even ignored.

The influence of Marxism-Leninism in the Third World dates perhaps from Lenin's *Imperialism: The Highest Stage of Capitalism,* which has influenced many millions who have not read the book but have some hearsay knowledge of its contents. They know that the book has been widely acclaimed and has influenced countless politicians, writers, and publications; that its author had made himself master of a world power; and that he wrote that capitalism can continue only by exploiting the rest of the world. The insubstantial ideas of that book and of many of its successors continue to be extremely influential and to serve as a source of Third World hostility to the market.[14]

Exploitation

The doctrine of exploitation, especially of Western exploitation of the Third World, has been a significant factor in the appeal of Marxist-Leninist ideology in less-developed countries.[15] It derives from the wider notion that property incomes, business incomes, and trading incomes are extracted from other people rather than earned by the recipients. This long-standing misconception has gained wide currency in the Third World and is often compounded with the doctrine of imperialism.[16] Many local politicians find it useful to insist that the prosperity of the West has been achieved at the expense of the Third World generally and their own country in particular. The suggestion helps to explain away a country's failure to meet political promises, such as prosperity, after decolonization.

To Marxists, property incomes imply exploitation and service industries are regarded as unproductive. In many less-developed countries, the principal agents of material progress have been external contacts, ethnic minorities, expatriate personnel, and foreign investments. Ethnic minorities have often enjoyed above-average incomes, usually from trade and related activities. The emotional and political appeal of the notion that the incomes of the relatively well-to-do are somehow extracted rather than earned and produced is exceptionally strong when those who are well-to-do are members of an ethnic or religious minority.

The notion of external exploitation has particular appeal because it effectively stirs up guilt feelings in the West and results in significant political and financial benefits to Third World govern-

73

ments. If Western profits are produced by exploitation, the expropriation of foreign enterprises is not only justified but even necessary to protect the population from exploitation and to make the country truly independent.

Western Guilt

A widespread feeling of guilt led the West also to accept, often subconsciously, the idea of Western exploitation of the Third World. Especially in America, acceptance of the idea has been assisted by the belief in the natural equality of man and by an unhistorical approach to the study of economic and social situations. If we believe that all are inherently equal, and also that history is bunk, then we are likely to accept the notion that income differences are evidence that some malevolent force has perverted the natural course of events.

The media, the arts, and the academies direct a ceaseless flow of allegations about Western guilt to the less-developed world, thus encouraging hostility to the market. Quite apart from straight exploitation through foreign investment, the operation of the market allegedly thrusts unwanted Western goods on the Third World, destroys or inhibits local industries for the benefit of the West, pollutes the environment, depletes resources, promotes inequality, erodes tradition (or, alternatively, helps traditional rulers to repress the population if that serves as a more effective accusation in the context). External market forces supposedly also damage less-developed countries by inflicting on them unfavorable and persistently deteriorating terms of trade, and also by bringing about wide fluctuations in their export prices and earnings. These ideas originate in the West and readily germinate and multiply in the Third World. These ideas are altogether insubstantial; external contacts have been prime agents in the development of many poor countries.[17]

These allegations treat the Third World as if it were a uniform, homogeneous collectivity, the component parts of which have identical interests which are opposed only to those of the West. These allegations have also encouraged the practice of worldwide aggregation and averaging of incomes, terms of trade, and other concepts and magnitudes that obscure the enormous diversity of physical, social, and economic conditions within the less-developed world. The outlook it promotes is that both domestic and international differences in income and wealth are abnormal and reprehensible and reflect market inadequacies; therefore, large-scale, coercive reduction of income differences is both feasible and desirable.

Official foreign aid also serves as an independent source of hostility to the market.[18] Since the aid is given to governments, it strengthens the position of and enlarges the state sector as compared to the private sector. It also serves as a source of money and patronage. In practice, the influence of foreign aid in promoting government-controlled economies is reinforced by the criteria of allocation, which favor governments trying to establish such economies. This accords with the prescriptions of academic economists, especially in the United States, for the determination of these criteria. They are reinforced further by the influence of opponents of the market in the administration and local distribution of aid.

Foreign aid also assists the politicization of life, that is, the tendency to make everything a matter of politics, and the politicization of life provokes and exacerbates political tension, which again arouses hostility to the market, especially in multiracial societies. Many recipient governments engaged in wholesale socialization have expelled ethnic minorities and other economically productive but politically ineffective groups. Altogether, official aid is, in practice, an important anti-market force.

MARKET FAILURES AND ECONOMIC CONTROLS

Poverty and Advance

Paradoxically, both the material poverty of less-developed countries and the frequent instances of rapid advance have been used to promote hostility to the market. Articulate groups both in the West and in the Third World often adduce the comparative poverty of less-developed countries as evidence of the failure of the market to secure development and prosperity, a failure said to be exacerbated by external exploitation. From these misdiagnoses, they infer the need for comprehensive planning, wholesale politicization of life, expropriation of foreign and domestic enterprises, or even enforced collectivization of farming.

As a further paradox, the rapid advances of recent decades in many Third World countries have often prompted a climate hostile to the market. There has been rapid advance in many parts of Asia, Africa, and Latin America, very largely as a result of contacts established with the West. But, though rapid, the advance has often been very uneven; it has affected some groups and regions sooner and more pervasively than others, causing considerable political and social strains. The tensions have been exacerbated by the greater ability of some groups and individuals to adapt to changing conditions and to seize the emerging economic opportunities. The causes of these various social and political tensions come to be attributed to the market system, which plays into the hands of its opponents.

Market Risks

Another source of hostility to the market is the belief that economic controls are necessary to shield people from the risks of the market, especially price fluctuations of export crops. Sometimes this belief is related to sentimental notions about the operation of a near-subsistence economy. Such

77

an economy, although it operates at a low level, is thought to be secure or snug. This is a misconception. Famines and the worst epidemic and endemic diseases occur in subsistence economies, not in market economies, because the former are very poor, have no accumulated reserves, and have no access to external resources and reserves. But although the hazards of subsistence economy are much more severe than those of a market economy, they are more readily accepted because they appear unavoidable and the causes seem obvious and certainly not man-made. On the other hand, the causes of economic reverses in a market economy—such as, say, a fall in export prices or a rise in retail prices—are more remote, more plausibly attributed to human malice and incompetence, and therefore more suspect. Thus, price fluctuations are more often thought to present a case for state control than fluctuations in crops, even though the latter cause greater hardship.

The idea that the population needs to be shielded from the hardships of price fluctuations has served as justification for the establishment of state export monopolies with the sole right to buy the crops. In many Asian and African countries these bodies have for many years paid the farmers a fraction of the market prices of the products, thereby taxing away the bulk of their incomes. This has retarded the expansion of the exchange economy and restricted the volume of private saving, thus inhibiting the emergence of a local capitalist class. At the same time, even the very modest incomes left in the hands of the farmers have often fluctuated widely as a result of the vagaries of official policy.

State controls have not secured stability in any meaningful sense for the farmers or other economic agents subject to them. Both controls and the consequent politicization of life involve hazards more severe and less predictable than those of the market. After all, if agricultural prices fluctuate, it is possible for producers (or, for that matter, governments) to set aside reserves. No such protection is available against the withdrawal of a trading license, the confiscation of income or property, or deportation.

The Unsystematic Market

References to planning often confuse or identify the idea of foresight in private or business conduct with government control of economic activity, that is, replacement of individual decisions by government decisions in economic activity. Actual or attempted state control of economic activity outside subsistence production has become the standard interpretation of planning in Third World development policy.

Planning thus interpreted has obvious appeal to politicians, administrators, and intellectuals, since it creates positions of power that members of these groups expect to fill, with resulting political, emotional, and financial advantages. A further source of appeal is the misconception that planning replaces an irrational and confused system by one based on method, reason, and science. This appeal is enhanced further if planning is linked to the all-embracing messianic creed of Marxism-Leninism. This linkage is especially important in the Third World, where the literati feel much superior to the rest of the population, while at the same time regretting their isolation. Economic controls do not solve either the very real emotional problems of the alienated intellectuals nor the real or alleged problems of market failure. But this does not detract from the *ex ante* appeal of planning, particularly because people are rarely informed about the political implications and the social and economic results of comprehensive planning.

Business Interests

Local and expatriate businessmen, too, have frequently welcomed economic controls. People habitually and understandably wish to increase the scarcity value of their services by curbing actual or potential competitors. Academic economists often blame businessmen for supporting restrictions or seeking direct subsidies, thus enfeebling or even undermining the market system, supposedly against their own interests, especially their own long-term interests. These charges bypass the central problem. If people pursue their immediate interests they must be expected to do so consistently. Support for restrictionism need not be short-sighted, since neither the immediate cost nor the ultimate consequences fall on those who support such measures. Indeed, it can be argued that directors or managers of businesses with outside shareholders fail in their duty if they do not support the restrictions advantageous to businesses they manage. As a result of the politicization of economic life, all too often under Western pressure, the prospects or even survival of businesses in less-developed countries often depend on political or administrative decisions. Vigorous or explicit resistance to restrictionism in the Third World is often economically damaging to businessmen and may even be economic suicide.

Analogous considerations apply to the failure of businessmen to resist academic and media hostility to the market. Effective action to influence the climate of opinion is difficult, expensive, complex, and often also requires reflection and some subtlety. It is in the nature of the market system that decision-making is diffused and in this sense the system is fragmented. The cost of attempts to influence opinion on a general issue falls on the particular business. Any benefit is conjectural, delayed, diffuse, and rarely compensates those who bear the cost. Moreover, in a market system, resources accrue to people who are efficient in the performance of specific functions, a capacity very different from the understanding of abstract ideas and concepts. A more valid charge against the conduct of businessmen in this area is their undiscriminating attitude toward ideas and their purveyors, which leads them to extend massive support to deter-

81

mined and effective opponents of the market.

Relevant to this discussion, one curious contrast between a market system and a socialist system deserves notice. The market system delivers the goods people want, but its supporters do not manage to explain why; the socialist system does not deliver the goods, but its supporters are very good at explaining why it does not, cannot, or even should not, do so. One system is long on desired goods and short on effective arguments; the other is short on desired goods but long on effective arguments.

A brief summary may be appropriate now.
1. In many less-developed countries the politicization of economic life has vastly increased the stakes in and the intensity of the fight for political power. Such a situation inevitably provokes political tension, especially in multiracial societies. As a result, communities that have coexisted for generations or even centuries have turned against each other. Moreover, the energies and activities of ambitious and resourceful men have come to be diverted from economic activity to politics and administration, sometimes by choice but quite often by necessity, since economic or even physical survival has come to depend on political developments and administrative decisions.

    In many less-developed countries, government controls have also restricted occupational and geographical mobility within the country. The results of the restrictions on external contacts and on domestic mobility are generally harmful to economic development. External contacts and the movement of people are prime agents in promoting peaceful, uncoerced change in ideas and mores, including the spread of new methods of production, new crops, new wants, and the attitudes, habits, and conduct congenial to material advance.

2. The preponderance of opponents of the market in the external intellectual, academic, and official contacts of the Third World with the West has been a major factor promoting hostility to the market. The international organizations have played a key role in this process.

3. The role of ideas and ideologies as a source of hostility to the market in the Third World has been compounded by misleading, loose, and loaded terminology. For instance, the less-developed countries are habitually described as "deprived" and "underprivileged." But people cannot be deprived of something they never had. The term serves to suggest that the West has caused the poverty of the Third World. "Underprivileged" is a nonsense expression. Privilege denotes officially conferred favors officially denied to others. All those not in receipt of such privilege can be described as

underprivileged. Thus, this term is a self-contradiction, an expression akin to "under-overfed."

We have also accepted much too readily the term "distribution of income." Incomes (other than subsidies) are not distributed but earned, that is, produced. There is no world distribution of income; there are only incomes produced in the numerous different societies of the world. Finally, in this context, as in others, we should talk about income *differences*, not *inequalities*. The former term is neutral; the latter implicitly prejudges the issue. This again stands out starkly on the international plane.

4. The military, political, and economic resources of most less-developed countries are meager or even negligible. Yet, these resources yield considerable political power on the world scene. Indeed, the West often abases itself before countries with no resources to speak of. This loss of nerve largely reflects a widespread but unfounded guilt feeling in the West. The guilt derives chiefly from the idea that the prosperity of the West has been extracted from the Third World, an instance of the pernicious misconception that incomes of the relatively better-off have been achieved at the expense of the relatively poor, that is, that the economic process is a zero sum game.

5. Hostility to the market is often closely allied to hostility to the West. Many people who insist that the West has caused the poverty of the Third World, whether through colonialism or the operation of the market, belong to disaffected and disenchanted groups in the West who treat less-developed countries as useful instruments to promote their own concerns in a civil conflict within the West. The abolition of the market system is their primary object. Though professing concern for the Third World, these people support policies that result in massive and acute hardship and suffering in the Third World, as shown, for instance, by the fate of the Asian minorities in Africa. More generally, the Western support indispensable to governments that pursue brutal and inhuman policies, the principal victims of which are Third World people, is often spurred by a feeling of guilt, or at any rate accompanied by expressions of guilt. But the feeling of guilt is rarely matched by a sense of responsibility for the policies it inspires.

6. The West often supports the people opposed to it or dedicated to its destruction. A large volume of virulent anti-Western and anti-market literature on the Third World and on its external contacts emanates from politicians, academics, and publicists, heavily supported by Western governments, in-

ternational organizations, or Western foundations. This literature includes travesties of history, evident economic misconceptions, and simple lapses. The extreme character of some of this literature and the extent of the dependence of the authors on Western support are apt to be ignored. Unfortunately, neither the political thrust nor the patent shortcomings of these publications have diminished either the support enjoyed by their authors or the effectiveness of the publications in promoting hostility both to the West and to the market system.

FOOTNOTES

1. In recent and current parlance, most of Africa, Asia, and Latin America have come to be lumped together, on the basis of a low level of conventionally measured incomes, as less-developed countries, the less-developed world, or the Third World. This terminology and the worldwide aggregation of profoundly diverse components is misleading and objectionable. I cannot avoid this infelicitous terminology on the present occasion. Its shortcomings do not affect the substantive argument.

I shall use the term "source of hostility to the market" to denote both certain ideas, attitudes, and conditions, and also organizations and institutions promoting this hostility. I hope it will be clear from the specific context what kind of influence is under discussion.

2. Throughout this paper, reference to international organizations is to official intergovernmental organizations.

3. *Development and Underdevelopment* (Cairo: National Bank of Egypt, 1956), p. 63.

4. *An International Economy* (London: Routledge and Kegan Paul, 1956), p. 201.

5. *Quiet Crisis in India* (Washington: The Brookings Institution, 1962), p. 28. The context of Professor Lewis' statement is development planning in India. The suggestion that the government's maintenance of a growth perspective, whatever that means, is the only indispensable condition of economic development cannot possibly be true. Professor Lewis, formerly Distinguished Service Professor of Economics at Indiana University and director of its International Development Research Center, established with the help of the Ford Foundation, subsequently became Dean of the Woodrow Wilson School at Princeton.

6. *The Economics of Underdeveloped Countries* (London: Weidenfeld and Nicholson, World University Library, 1966), p. 244. Professor Bhagwati, an economist of international standing, is a full professor of economics at the Massachusetts Institute of Technology. Formerly full professor at Delhi, he has been on a number of international missions. The book from which I quote was published in many countries.

7. That these groups also disassociate themselves from local and visiting market-oriented academics affects the prestige and effectiveness even of academics of standing who are well-prepared and who know the local scene. My own experience is that, if the visitor is well-prepared, this is often less important than might appear.

It happens, however, that market-oriented visitors are often insufficiently prepared. In particular, they do not know the local scene well, and this can be damaging. Market opponents can get away with shortcomings that are not forgiven in market supporters.

8. Witness the passages by Professor Myrdal quoted earlier.

9. Primary examples are widespread licensing of economic activity and government trading monopolies, including export monopolies for agricultural products. The latter were introduced virtually throughout British Africa and Burma and a number of other territories but did not have significant monopoly power in export markets. They had and still have monopoly of the purchase of crops subject to them, that is monopsony power over the producers.

10. Perceptive and explicit observations on this subject by early colonial administrators are quoted in my book *Dissent on Development* (Cambridge, Mass.: Harvard University Press, 1972), especially essay 14, "Background to Exodus."

11. It is a moot point whether in this context the less-developed countries are regarded more appropriately as allies or instruments. They are allies in that their spokesmen are articulate, especially when they express opinions derived from the West or when they are briefed from the West. But their resources are often so meager and so largely derived from the West that they may be regarded as instruments. But frequent and often evident lack of concern of their champions in the West for the consequences of many policies in the Third World supported by them also suggests that they look on the peoples of less-developed countries as instruments rather than as allies; see the concluding section of this paper.

12. In 1958 I asked a highly educated and very helpful Indian economist in Delhi about legislation that prohibited the slaughter of cows or even of all cattle in most major Indian States, including the largest. Although this legislation was common knowledge and widely publicized in the Indian press (but for many years not reported in the West), he first denied its existence and then his knowledge of it. On being questioned further, he virtually broke down and begged me

not to remind him of his isolation from the vast majority of his countrymen.

13. This factor in the appeal of Marxism-Leninism is a theme of a penetrating study by Czeslaw Milosz, *The Captive Mind* (London: Secker and Warburg, 1953).

14. See, for example, the passages from the prominent academics Paul A. Baran and Peter Townsend cited in my "Western Guilt and Third World Poverty," *Commentary,* January 1976.

15. In much current discussion the people of less-developed countries have come to be regarded as a proletariat, which is by definition exploited. In fact, most people there are small-scale farmers, not workers employed by capitalists.

16. Thus, in the context of the Third World the idea of exploitation as a cause of backwardness is primarily Leninist rather than Marxist; Marx was rather explicit in recognizing the role of capitalism in promoting material progress in backward societies.

17. The role of external contacts in the development of many poor countries is discussed in my article "Western Guilt and Third World Poverty," *Commentary,* January 1976.

18. All references to foreign aid are to official intergovernmental economic aid.

4

A Comment on "Hostility to the Market in Less Developed Countries"

Nathan Glazer

Two themes sounded strongly in Peter Bauer's paper encourage me to extend his perceptive and powerful analysis of the dynamics of market hostility in the less-developed countries. I must repeat here his necessary precaution—that the great variety of countries in the Third World gives the appearance of overgeneralization to almost any comment one might make. Nevertheless, generalizations, taking into account the endless exceptions and glosses each would require, carry some persuasion.

The first theme in Professor Bauer's paper on which I would like to expand is presented early and is often adverted to: "much of the hostility emanating from the Third World originates in the West." Ideas about economies and economics, we all realize, are not automatically derived from experience or from traditional folk wisdom; or, if they are to some extent derived from these sources, these are not the main ways they are shaped. Ideas about economics involve large abstractions about matters not generally part of the traditional concerns of the less-developed countries before Western contact, and thus they must be derived from some process of education different from the transmission of folk or traditional knowledge. They require books, newspapers, schools, universities, elaborated discourse. In this respect, ideas about economics are not very different from, let us say, ideas about the solar system or medicine. There may be a folk component in them, but in the underdeveloped world, as in the developed world, the folk and traditional component in shaping ideas about such matters has been quite overwhelmed by a much larger element coming from the West. There is a strong line of connection thus, important in explaining the sources of market hostility in less-developed countries, between the economic ideas of the intellectuals, political leaders, educators, journalists, radio commentators, and other people of influence in the Third World in the transmission of ideas and the West, which must be the source of ideas in such an area as the workings of the economy, as it is the source of the institutions and technical mechanisms whereby these ideas are transmitted.

Here we come upon an oddity (and there are many more). First, in the developed world, it is that part which has (to the extent any part of the world has) a free market and free political institutions that is overwhelmingly the source of the ideas that influence the developing world. It is not Moscow that shapes the ideas of Third World leaders, teachers, intellectuals, and the like; it is Paris, Rome, and New York. This is not to say that Moscow (and Peking and Havana) are without influence, but their influence, I would judge, is more political and military than directly intellectual. Or, it is an influence by the power of example (to which we may add, even more strongly, Peking and Havana). But it is Western intellectuals—using that term to apply to the free-market-oriented and democratic part of the world—who interpret for the intellectuals of the less-developed countries the supposed economic success of Communist countries and, more significantly, explicate the variety of reasons that one should oppose the market and democratic institutions.

Thus, whatever the success of Moscow in the Third World in distributing books of Marxist classics and Marxist literature in economics, it is not my impression that this vast propaganda flow has much *direct* influence in shaping economic ideas in less-developed countries. As Professor Bauer points out, it is the Western advisors, teachers, and employees of international organizations who are the chief sources of the teaching of hostility to the market. The interpreters of Marx or of other socialists who are influential in the Third World are more likely English, French, or American than Russian (or Chinese or Cuban).

THE INFLUENCE OF WESTERN
UNIVERSITIES

There are obvious reasons for this relative weakness of the Communist countries in being a direct source for the diffusion of ideas. The majority of Third World leaders, teachers, intellectuals, and the like have been educated in the democratic capitalist countries, if they have been educated abroad; the curriculums of the local universities in these countries are shaped by influences from Western capitalist countries, teachers and administrators from them. The foreign languages spoken and read by leaders and intellectuals in the less-developed countries are English and French, not Russian. One need not go further than this in trying to explain why the Western sources of hostility to the market are to be found in the free market and democratic countries, rather than in those countries that have suppressed the market.

There is a second oddity when we consider this line of influence more closely. The dominant economic ideas in the field of economics for decades now in the West have been based on the analysis of the free market and explicitly or implicitly have argued its virtues for efficiency, investment decisions, economic growth, and the like. Where in the Western universities—which are the major source of ideas on economics which influence students from the developing world—do we find any substantial concentration of market opponents? One may mention the names of Paul Baran, John

Kenneth Galbraith, Gunnar Myrdal, Joan Robinson, et al., but really it appears that the weight of the profession and of the popularizers of economic ideas has been with the supporters of the free market; even some of those who may be quoted in opposition are not *determined* supporters of statism, but merely supporters of some degree of state intervention in an economic system which they think on the whole should be market-controlled.

We deal here, I am convinced, with a real mystery. The sources of market hostility in the Third World are in the West and the market hostility of the developed Western world is internally generated. But where and how are these ideas generated when the economic profession is controlled by persons who believe in the efficacy of the market, the textbooks for colleges and secondary schools are dominated by these persons, and the newspapers, insofar as they present economic ideas, are, generally speaking, more biased in favor of the market than against it?

I do not know if others are as mystified by this phenomenon as I am, but let me give you my personal reason for finding this mystifying. About ten years ago, if one examined the field of American sociology, ideas parallel to and related to the market emphasis in economics dominated. Generally, teachers assigned Marx as reading material only to point out that what he was saying was monistic, naïve, time-bound, limited, and that his ideas had to be supplemented by the more complex and pluralistic ideas of Max Weber and other sociologists.

C. Wright Mills and Alvin Gouldner were the only major American sociologists who were Marxists. There were few avowed or unavowed Marxists teaching sociology and, though there were many socialists and ex-socialists, even these were democratic socialists, pluralist in political outlook, only mild supporters of state intervention for some given purposes in the economy, eclectic in social thinking. In any case, there were no believers in the absolute dominance of a ruling class owning the means of production and no believers in the Marxist and radical socialist analyses that are hostile to diversity and freedom in social life.

There has been a remarkable transformation in ten years or so. Younger teachers of sociology are now completely different from *their* teachers and one wonders where they got their ideas. Students of sociology at Harvard today, in a department in which there are no Marxists or radical socialists among the senior faculty, are concerned with justifying, if not Marx, at least Marxism, or neo-Marxism, and find their sustenance and support in French and German—being students they must show some originality—Marxist or neo-Marxist writers who are not assigned in their classes and whom they discover on their own.

There is an interesting process here, akin to that process by which leaders and intellectuals of the Third World got many of their ideas—not from reading the assigned texts, going to the assigned lectures, or reading the major newspapers. They sought out the ideas they wanted—in informal study groups, meetings of small radical groups, obscure weekly newspapers, monthly "theoretical" magazines, and the like. It is not the case, I believe, that there has been a dominant strain of hostility to the market in the universities and colleges of the Western world in their "official" teaching. There have undoubtedly been such teachers, but the career of Paul Baran shows they have had their difficulties and, even if they have not, they have been countered by far more numerous market supporters. I have in mind the imbalance in the Harvard economics department, which would undoubtedly be considered one of the more liberal ones—the opponents of the market make up perhaps two out of twenty. I suspect the proportions in general are not very different elsewhere. In sociology, which I know somewhat better, I would argue that there is a complete reversal in ideas when we move from the generation of the older teachers—those in their fifties and sixties—to the present generation of young teachers—those in their twenties and thirties.

Yes, the hostility to the market in less-developed countries—as in the West itself—stems from the West, but I would argue that its own sources in the West are not so clear. These ideas do not reflect the dominant thinking and teaching in the universities and colleges, but are only becoming so as young people, who got their ideas from no official channel, come to dominance in them. This phenomenon affects areas outside the colleges and universities. The mass media, once considered pillars of the market, are now to be considered, I would judge, at best neutral. Consider the change in the ordinary and casual assumptions of writers in *Time* and *Newsweek* and of commentators in radio and television over the past ten years. The defenders of the market, feeling their power ebbing, now take on a querulous tone; they sound like extremists in a society supposedly dominated by the free market and its supporters. I would suggest you tune in on some radio talk shows and check the balance of querulousness and shrillness between the defenders of the free market and free market institutions and those who are critical of them. David Brudnoy, an official conservative commentator on a Boston radio station, sounds more extreme than any democratic socialist would and I would hazard that James Kilpatrick sounds more extreme than Shana Alexander.

THE POWER OF DISSENT

We are not without considerable aid in understanding this phenomenon: the work of Lewis Feuer on the political conflicts of generations, of Joseph Schumpeter on the sources of intellectuals' hostility to capitalism, Daniel Bell's recent writing collected in his book *The Cultural Contradictions of Capitalism,* and some perceptive essays by Irving Kristol. This is not the place for a full analysis of the writings that help us understand why a generation may turn against its teachers or how capitalism creates its own destroyers. Even these im-

98

portant contributions to understanding this phenomenon I find not fully satisfying, because we deal not only with a secular trend but with a peculiarly sharp reversal in popular ideas and of thinking—a reversal for which there is little support in the dominant or official sources of ideas in the past ten years. Undoubtedly, we would have to refer to some specific historical developments, too, to explain what is happening: the Vietnam war, the success of Cuba in stabilizing itself and the supposed success of China in dealing with some of the most difficult problems of the Third World (population control, the establishment of a sound national health system, food production, income distribution).

What I find most appealing in the possible explanations for what has happened leads me to a second theme in Professor Bauer's paper, one on which I will comment much more briefly: the isolation felt by Western-educated (and indeed locally educated) intellectuals and leaders from their own people in the less-developed countries. Professor Bauer writes, "These situations predispose the intellectuals and the educated classes to an all-embracing creed, especially one that promises emotional integration or reintegration with their fellowmen." Undoubtedly this isolation is a far more serious matter in the less-developed countries, where huge gaps separate the educated and influential from the rest of the population, than in the West, where we find lesser discontinuities in income, education, and power, from the top to the

99

bottom of society. And yet the attractiveness of an ideology which promises this emotional reintegration is very powerful in the West, too, for somewhat different reasons. In the West, the attraction of this ideology relates to the fact that social institutions that integrate people—villages, rural communities, families, family businesses, and the like —have either almost disappeared or have undergone great transformation. Perhaps, thus, the force of this desire for reintegration in the West comes from the abstraction of a partially remembered or imagined community of the past and the promise of a reintegrating ideology to build a new community in the future, in which the integrating bonds would derive not from tradition and communal controls but from the state. In the less-developed countries there is a real and startling gap between intellectuals and ordinary people in the present; in the West this gap is much smaller. Thus, when intellectuals, students, journalists, and writers in the West accept an ideology, as they are accepting the ideologies critical and destructive of the market, they paradoxically have a much greater chance of influencing the rest of the society—first, because they make up so much of it, and second, because the whole society is so much more closely knit, through mass media, formal education, and the like.

These comments have, I know, scarcely thrown much light on the phenomenon we are analyzing. My objective, however, has been to emphasize how *strange* this phenomenon is, strange particularly when considered by people who themselves find nothing appealing in it. The fact is that a suppressed ideology, the ideology of Marxism and hostility to the market—suppressed because its opponents had more money and power, suppressed by governments in much of the world at different times, suppressed by, to my mind, the success of more complex alternative views of the world which bested Marxism in the free competition of ideas in a free world—has shown a remarkable resilience, in the less-developed countries and in the West; while the ideas we prefer, those that show the superiority of the free market, despite the fact that they have not (aside from the Communist world) been actively suppressed by the government, seem to have little appeal. What we might consider an underground ideology shows remarkable vitality, despite the fact that it is wrong; ideas we consider much closer to the truth show remarkable weakness, even though (aside from the Communist world) they have the right to circulate freely, they have the at least pusillanimous support of governments, and they have the stronger support of at least one major institution with power and wealth—business. That the suppressed should flourish and the approved and supported should decline—this is, indeed, mystifying, particularly when truth is not on the side of the underground ideology. It will take all our wit and ingenuity in research to understand this phenomenon and to

101

add further to the understanding and insight that those who have been dealing with it—Professor Bauer and some of the others I have mentioned—have already given us.

5

Some Irrational Sources of Opposition to the Market System

Lewis S. Feuer

A duality of motivation characterizes human nature, such that every social system somehow must accommodate itself to both the affectional and aggressive drives of people. The unparalleled achievement of the competitive capitalist society rests on a psychological fact: it was the first to channel man's aggressive drives into constructive uses. Previously, aggressive drives were mainly expressed through war, conquest, plunder, and enslavement; these drives always went hand in hand with the destruction of societies, communities, and people. Sometimes a society or group, filled with revulsion against these warlike, cruel manifestations, would turn its aggressions inward to search for an affectional, cooperative life combined with a self-aggressive, self-punitive asceticism. But capitalist society rechanneled these aggressive energies into constructive and creative activity. In seeking to profit, it helped raise people's standard of living. The business elite was, moreover, friendly to the inventors of new processes, machines, and objects; the inventors took delight in the knowledge that they had mastered the environment and their labor-saving devices had outmaneuvered the intent of any self-punitive religion of guilt.

To many persons, however, the capitalist system seemed to impose a heavy burden on the affectional component of human nature. "Commercialism, competition, has sown the wind recklessly, and must reap the whirlwind," wrote William Morris. He looked upon the middle classes as a force "so terrible that I think it not unlikely that their resistance to inevitable change may . . . ruin all civilization for a time." Workingmen striving to rise into the middle class meant "multiplying the capitalist class (every member of which you must remember is engaged in fierce private commercial war with his fellows) . . ."[1] The competition and poverty of the unskilled laborers in England in 1884 appalled Morris so much that he said it "makes one ashamed to live."[2]

That every society, including the competitive capitalist society, must take such structural measures that will allow for the satisfaction of the affectional side of man seems to me an axiom of politics. But the widespread critiques of the free market society, though claiming to be founded on a desire to satisfy repressed affectional longings, often proceed from other drives, even crypto-aggressive ones. The socialist reformer may be concerned less

104

with socialism than with projecting aggressive impulses into a struggle against the system.

How can we distinguish the rationally motivated person from the irrationally motivated one? Whenever a person chooses disproportionate means to achieve a given end, an irrational motive may be at work. This is the case with a worker who calls for a strike in response to some minor incident or with a person who reacts to a paltry boundary dispute with a call for war. A second sort of irrational behavior concerns not the choice of means, but the end itself. An end that is self-destructive is irrational, as, for example, the miser's accumulation of coins. These two varieties of irrational action blend into one. The person who chooses disproportionate means does so because an unavowed, unconscious end dictates those means; thus, the person who chooses violence or cruelty to achieve a given political reform may do so because he wants the violence or cruelty, which are his real ends, rather than his avowed end of political reform. Psychological analysis reveals that means-disproportionality is usually behavior determined by an unconscious, unavowed end. However, an unconsciously determined end might also be a rational one, as, for instance, a scientist's love for truth. Only in those instances in which, having become conscious of an underlying unconscious end, we reject it as destructive of other, more highly prized ends, can we judge the rejected end to be irrational. An irrational source of objection to the free market, then, is one which is founded on

105

largely repressed or unconscious feelings which contravene the person's basic conscious values.

From the purely economic standpoint, there are both rational and irrational sources of opposition to the free market. An unemployed worker in 1932 in the midst of the Great Depression, willing to work for even subsistence wages, but finding no jobs available and a pervasive spirit of defeat among businessmen, might well have concluded that the free market closed rather than opened opportunities for men. But, curiously, the rational criticism of the capitalist society has been far less influential in recent years than the one derived from irrational grounds, from premises that are not articulated.

THE DIALECTICAL PERSONALITY OF OUR TIME

Hostility to the free market was not founded on a claim that the competitive capitalist system no longer worked. In the 1960s, the most influential antagonists of the free market conceded, almost without exception, that it does work: it provides ample livelihoods and comforts to the vast majority of people. Thus, the arguments of writers such as Erich Fromm, Herbert Marcuse, and Paul Goodman became prophetic moral denunciations. Erich Fromm found that the competitive capitalist society bred warped characters—exploitative, passive, hoarding; the market, he alleged, was an arena in which men's personalities engaged in

106

gladiatorial combat and could never become truly "productive." Herbert Marcuse saw the working class as a collectivity which had been stupefied by capitalism with "administered comforts"; he looked, therefore, to intellectuals to inaugurate the "explosion" of the capitalist society. To all these writers, the word "alienation" has been central; it is their master metaphor. The young Marx and Engels had written that in capitalist society, the cash nexus reduces and debases all human relations—love, work, and culture—into saleable commodities. Alienated labor, in the form of goods and capital, said Marx, stands over man rather than serves him; it severs his connection with nature. According to Fromm, likewise, the free market estranges people from themselves so that they do not experience themselves as subjects, as the centers of their world, as creators of their acts, but as objects, as peripheral satellites to others, as creatures,[3] not creators.

This psychological criticism of the free market system, part of the sociological common sense of our time, needs reassessment and revision. We need to understand its sources. Such psychologists of the unconscious as Erich Fromm and Herbert Marcuse have never felt the need to analyze the type of personality of which they themselves are such noted examples—we might call it "the dialectical personality of our time." Its character traits determine the preconceptions and the terminology of their critique of capitalist society. The dialectical personality is moved by a compulsive spirit of contrariety; he wishes, in a favorite Marxist metaphor, to stand things on their head; he is fond of the imagery of birth and the womb; each society is pregnant with its opposite; and force is the midwife of history. The word "dialectical" is chosen to describe this devotion to "contradiction" as the vocation of man and history. The system must be inexorably "negated"; "negation" is indeed endowed by such writers with a special emotional valence. To the Rev. Norman Vincent Peale's "The Power of Positive Thinking," Prof. Herbert Marcuse counterposes The Power of Negative Thinking. (He has written a book called *Negations.*) They wish not only to "negate" the free market, but to "negate" its abstractional and mathematical traits and to "negate" the physical and economic science which has been developed with these instruments.

There are various types of dialectical personalities. Karl Marx, George Bernard Shaw, Thorsten Veblen, Erich Fromm, and Herbert Marcuse are examples of one type. Educated as literary intellectuals, these men regarded entry into the competitive market as a traumatic and degrading experience. Usually the children of a protective family with an aesthetic or religious atmosphere, they grew up estranged from commerce and industry and hostile to its values.

Herbert Marcuse, for instance, "the scion of an upper-class Jewish family prominent in Berlin society since the eighteenth century," attended uni-

108

versities, became adept in phenomenological and existential philosophy, studied under Martin Heidegger, and joined a student socialist group.[4] He was happiest in Frankfurt in the only Marxist research institute in the bourgeois world (financed by a German-Argentine grain merchant).

Erich Fromm, descended from "a long rabbinical background," found the Old Testament writings most congenial, especially those of the prophets Isaiah, Amos, and Hosea. Perhaps no group of ancient writers was so anti-commercial, anti-liberal, and anti-scientific. The wisdom of Proverbs or Ecclesiastes does not seem to have attracted Fromm. The consequence of such an education was that he was trained to be "somewhat a stranger in the modern world."[5]

A similar religious longing drove Karl Marx to a life of stormy self-sacrifice. He too elected a course on Isaiah at the university and dedicated himself to Hegel and ancient philosophy. Sickened though he was by the vapid, pretentious unreality of Hegelian metaphysics, he recognized that it was the ideology of the young university intellectuals and he was determined to share "modernity" with them. He lived on his father's money, his mother's money, his uncle's money, and his wife's family belongings and the money given him by his friend Friedrich Engels. To look for a job was for Marx a surrender to the capitalist system. His family starved, his wife and children were enfeebled, and several children died. Only once did Marx condescend to look for a job, but his illegible handwriting saved him from being hired as a railway clerk and from being drawn into what he regarded as bourgeois filth.

DISTASTE FOR EMPLOYMENT

The notion that looking for a job is demeaning and the expectation that one's family is obliged to finance one's cultural pursuits long into one's maturity are characteristic of the dialectical personality. Bernard Shaw used to boast that until he was thirty his mother supported him while he wrote unpublishable novels, read in the British Museum which he admired as the archetype of a socialist institution, and spoke at Fabian enclaves and Hyde Park open meetings on the irrationality of the market system.

Thorsten Veblen was probably the only doctor of philosophy in the United States in the 1880s who could not find a job. He sat on his father's farm in Minnesota for seven years, delving into the literature of social protest, Edward Bellamy's *Looking Backward,* Ferdinand Lassalle, and Marx. Finally, the family held a council and decided to send him back to graduate school.

The dialectical personality is not all book-loving; it has, invariably, a strong ingredient of sadism, in a curiously oscillating relationship with a sacrificial component. Marx, responding in 1856 to a toast, "The Proletarians of Europe," fell back on the vengeful imagery of a medieval secret tribunal, the *Vehmgericht,* which marked a red cross on

110

those whom it doomed: "All the houses of Europe are now marked by the mysterious red cross. History is the judge; its executioner, the proletarian."[6] Marx's self-assigned role was to render self-consciousness to the role of the judge and executioner. George Bernard Shaw, an advocate of absolute equality, proposed to enforce it by executing, with the utmost goodwill, all those who could not do their required work: "Long ago I suggested that we should all be obliged to appear before a Board (virtually an inquisition) every five years, and justify our existence to its satisfaction on the pain of liquidation." A stable civilization, Shaw insisted, cannot exist "without such an inquisitorial power"; he was also much impressed by "a humanely conducted convict settlement" he saw in Russia.[7] Veblen delighted in the end of democracy and representative government in Russia; all was justified so long as the single end was achieved: "the disallowance of Absentee Ownership"; the "insubstantial citizens" were disposing of the "substantial ones."[8] Veblen charged that America was affected by a collective case of "dementia praecox," but he, too, like Marx and Shaw, identified with the tribunal of history pronouncing the death-sentence: "Discontinuance of the rights of ownership is the equivalent to the 'day of judgment' for the regime of the elder statesmen . . ."[9]

The dialectical personality *qua* executioner of the world's history will obviously find more opportunities for satisfaction in a planned dictatorial society than in a competitive free one. Historical sadism has a greater stage when it controls all of the state's resources, its economic power and its judiciary. It is therefore inclined to abrogate the competitive free market with its polycentric distribution of power.

Most persons did not suffer a "trauma of the market" as dialectical personalities did. The latter perceived the free market as monstrous, as a threat to their manhood. They did not experience joy in the opportunity for initiative, invention, enterprise, the pleasure of independence, which the market brought to countless numbers. Many persons experienced these joys. In the eighteenth century such writers as Daniel Defoe extolled the market, the delight of English tradesmen in their businesses, and in what he called "projects." A "projecting humor," he wrote, was awakened in England around the year 1690. In the nineteenth century, Alexis de Tocqueville described how Americans left their families at such a young age that there was virtually no adolescence in America. They went from job to job, regarding each as an experiment in finding the work best suited to them. He described how they revelled in invention, in conceiving new commodities and technologies. Thomas A. Edison, as a boy of twelve, found adventure selling papers on a railway, building himself a laboratory, living the life of a wandering telegraph operator; the market to him was a great sounding-board for the needs of human

112

beings, and an intimation of the direction for human progress and invention, that helped inspire him to invent the phonograph and the motion picture.

There was nothing of this note of challenge in the critical intellectuals' outlook toward the market. In their adolescences, which sometimes dragged on into their thirties, they were still primarily imbibers of culture—Marcuse with his Hegel, Fromm with Judaica, Marx with metaphysics, Shaw with music, art, and literature, Veblen with Kant and socialist pamphlets. In a world in which science, industry, and commerce gained eminence, the literary intellectuals became ever more embittered.

SYSTEMATIC HATRED FOR CAPITALISM

From what inner psychological traits does this traumatic perception of the market arise? How do these traits affect the analysis of the free market? The emotional *a priori* or postulate of the dialectical personality is that whatever the social problem, no solution shall be possible in the capitalist system. Racial animosity, technical underdevelopment, defects in education, the tension between the sexes, the exhaustion of natural resources, or the damage to the environment—none of these problems can be solved within; indeed, they are exacerbated by capitalism.

In an essay he wrote in 1972 for a symposium on "Ecology and Revolution" in the leftist magazine

Liberation, Marcuse's imagery clearly expresses this "dialectical postulate." Why is he concerned with ecology, Marcuse asks? He answers:

> Because the *violation* of the Earth is a vital aspect of the counter-revolution. [my italics throughout]
>
> *Nature* was the very *negation* of the *market society*, with its values of profit and utility.
>
> Monopoly capitalism is waging *a war against nature*, human nature as well as external nature. For the demands of more intense *exploitation* come into conflict with *nature* itself . . .
>
> The structure of capitalist productivity is indirectly expansionist . . .
>
> The restoration of the Earth as a human environment . . . Authentic ecology flows into a militant struggle for a socialist politics which must attack the system at its roots . . .[10]

Marcuse's failure to raise the question "How has the natural environment fared under the planned socialist economy in the Soviet Union?" suggests that irrational, non-logical, non-scientific factors determine his writings on ecology and the free market. A huge body of evidence indicates that a socialist society is far more irresponsible toward the environment than a free capitalist society. In the Soviet Union, the managers who put production before its impact on the environment can always claim that they were not being selfish, but that they were acting on the Bolshevik model to fulfill the planning targets; their ministries invariably support them. "We are building socialism" is their excuse to the environmentalists. One Soviet

114

manager described the "contradiction" between the imperative of socialist production and the moral claim of the environment: "What about the plan? Are you going to order the plants to stop? That is the dialectic. One has to choose between civilization and one's love of nature."[11] Under the free market economy, on the other hand, there are more powerful self-corrective agencies to intervene on behalf of the environment. Consumers' groups, residents' groups, hikers' clubs, hotels in natural resorts, rival companies and industries whose interests are adversely affected by environmental damage, medical associations and scientific societies, denounce and indict the offending industries for inflicting irreparable harm upon the community and for imposing hidden social costs on their fellow citizens.

Legislation to safeguard against atmospheric pollution is increasingly enforced in the American free market economy; it is generally ignored in the Soviet planned economy. However, neither Marcuse nor his fellow ecological Marxists have analyzed the relative capacities of capitalist and socialist societies for dealing with environmental problems. Instead, they use a variety of emotive metaphors to ignite unconscious tensions and to mobilize them into aggression against the capitalist economy.

Thus, the capitalist system is depicted as the rapist of one's mother; the Earth, the universal maternal symbol, is being "violated." Monopoly capitalism, with its inherently expanding productivity (the son's imagery of the all-powerful father) "extends" itself into "the space for release and escape represented by nature" (again, the lustful father attacking the mother's feminine space where release and escape are to be found), in a war against both "human nature as well as external nature" (both the son and the mother). Exploitation in Marcuse's metaphors is both the feminization of the son and the rape of the mother. For the market society "civilizes" man by reducing him to an object; capitalism is the father who turns the son into an object, that is, he reifies him by emasculating him. Nature, the mother, remains as the "very negation" of the repressive paternal market society, with its utilitarian criteria. Yet the Earth, the mother, cannot be won by the son within the framework of capitalism; "ecological logic is . . . the negation of capitalist logic," that is, the son must destroy the father—it is not possible to reform the dominant paternal authority; it must be eliminated altogether.

The metaphors and imagery of the dialectical personality turn out to be those of a fixated generational rebellion; the youth master uses those images which arouse the unconscious resentments of their own fathers in young intellectuals, guiding them to redirect their feelings toward the struggle against the market system which, by projection, is said to emasculate, reify, and objectify them, with its whip of the cash nexus.

The dialectical personality thus projects the deepest personal unresolvable conflict of the

116

young upon the character of the social system. Thus, the dialectical personality's personal conflict becomes generalized; he tries to resolve his conflicts by overturning the social system; he looks to a revolutionary act to release the emotions frustrated in a personal context.[12]

Key elements in the indictment of the market system bear witness to such origins in the personal unconscious. Erich Fromm, for instance, like Marcuse, denounced the "abstractification" and "quantification" which prevails under modern capitalism. Dr. Fromm resents such statements as "Mr. Henry Ford produced so many automobiles."[13] Exactly why such quantification should be regarded as peculiar to the capitalist market is never made clear. Moses enumerated the Hebrews in their exodus from Egypt and the Book of Job sets forth the numbers of cattle and children with which Jehovah finally rewarded the steadfast man. Planned socialist economies quantify far more than capitalist ones; for instance, Soviet factories, workers, and their social relations are identified by number. To a considerable extent, quantification is necessary in any society in which arrangements have to be made that involve large numbers of people, and the classical writers on "political arithmetic," such as Sir William Petty, conceived of their statistical science as an aid to both human understanding and happiness. But Fromm and Marcuse play on the dislike which so many children feel for numbers and arithmetic, a dislike

117

which literary intellectuals retain. The child often regards numbers as part of the discipline imposed by a sometimes harsh and hostile adult world; numbers threaten the spontaneity of existence. The free market, with its numbered supply and demand, can become the projective target for resentment against the numbers that seemed to put an end to the child's soft, maternal world.

THE ROOT OF ALL EVIL

The child's trauma of money is also invoked by the dialectical personality. From Karl Marx to Erich Fromm, from Spartan to Soviet society, the critics of the free market have composed emotional polemics against money. Money, wrote Marx, was the "radical leveller" abolishing the qualitative distinctions among commodities, and therefore justly denounced by the ancients as subversive of the moral order of things; both in his middle-aged *Capital* and his youthful unpublished manuscripts, Marx quoted Shakespeare's invocation against money:

> Gold, yellow, glittering precious gold!
> Thus much of this, will make black white,
>   foul, fair,
> Wrong, right; base, noble; old, young; coward,
>   valiant . . .
> Will knit and break religions; . . .
> . . . Come damned earth,
> Thou common whore of mankind.[14]

Fromm too declares that the possession of money is an inhuman way of acquiring commodities: "The human way of acquiring would be to make an effort qualitatively commensurate with what I acquire."[15]

Every child does experience anxieties concerning exchange. Many well-known stories tell of the simple farmer's boy who kept exchanging his money and objects until finally he had practically nothing left; ignorant either of the labor theory of value or the relative quantities of labor-time incorporated into different objects, the unfortunate child in the fairy story fails to solve the equations of exchange. And every child in his first purchases wonders whether he should get some money back; he feels he is at the mercy of the adult merchant who dictates the terms of the trade and is defenseless against the cheater. The dialectical school rekindles this childhood trauma. It matters little that the invention of money was actually a tremendous advance in the history of human freedom, that it not only made possible a flexible exchange of goods, but by assisting in bourgeois calculation, helped make people rational; the desire to trade with all and sundry was often the most powerful counterweight to religious and tribal divergences. The dialecticians ignore the fact that when communist societies try to take account of the variety of human desires, they always reintroduce the institution of money.

The critics also suggest that the market trespasses on the sacred, that it indeed violates the

119

First Commandment. These sentiments often are expressed in a quasi-religious language. Thus, in Erich Fromm's writings, the free market is said to breed "idolatry or alienation." "The idol represents his own life forces in a alienated form"; it stands apart from men and against them, even though men built it. The dialecticians see the market as a kind of pagan god, a Moloch, built from people's labor, but in whose fires the builders will be destroyed.

Central to Fromm's definition of mental health in *The Sane Society* is the individual's "emergence from incestuous ties to clan and soil." The dialectical personality, however, tends not to extend such freedom to include independence from class, party, proletariat, movement, or revolution. For the revolutionary intellectuals have invested these terms with the same type of emotion that Fromm labels "incestuous." The annals of Marxism are filled with paeans to "the great heart of the working class," the Goddess of Revolution, and the nurturing bosom of the party. The vague indictment that "alienated labor separates man from nature" projects the unconscious resentment that "alienated labor" is the work which the father demands of the intellectual son, who hates to give up his art and play in order to make a living. Yet, most men strive for a separation or independence from a recurrently cruel and capricious nature: witness the houses they have built, the wells they have dug, the clothes they have sewn.

In short, the dialectical personality in his critique of the capitalist system projects a personal animus characteristic of fixated generational rebels rather than of humanity at large. The market is depicted as an impersonal, remorseless giant devouring human lives; the revolutionary intellectual is Jack the Giant Killer. So Fromm writes, "The giant state and economic system are not any more controlled by man"; he complains of "the laws of the market, like God's will . . . beyond the reach of your will and influence," and calls for the defiance of the "anonymity" of the capitalist forces.

THE CONVERGENCE OF NEUROSES

Marcuse, Fromm, and Paul Goodman became the senior prophetic figures for the student leftists and revolutionary intellectuals of the sixties. By the end of that decade, the dialectical personality had become more *modal* among the younger generation in the United States than it had ever been. The rejection of the market as an institution became an axiom for many students at a time when American economic power, capitalist stability, standards of living, and technological achievement were at their height. Contrary to Marx's predictions, the rate of profit was not falling and production continued to expand. The anti-capitalist fashion in the sixties clearly, then, had irrational sources. Certainly, many of the leading personalities in the student left have been documented as cases of extreme neuroses; the percentage of such neuroses, often of a most tragic kind, exceeds manyfold the known instances of such in the American radicalism of the thirties. To mention only a few well-known instances among American New Leftists—Mario Savio, the most eloquent of Berkeley's student leaders, whose name was a byword for the intransigent rejection of the "system," became a patient in a mental institution;[16] Robert Starobin, spokesman for Berkeley's graduate students in 1964–65, committed suicide in 1970;[17] Marshall Bloom of Amherst, who was the principal agent in closing the London School of Economics for the academic year 1966–67, committed suicide in 1969;[18] Jerry Rubin, who went from Berkeley leadership in 1966 to the Chicago Seven of 1968, was in 1975 the devotee of a bizarre cult of the self-adoration of the body;[19] while his colleague in disruption, Rennie Davis, had taken the robes of a missionary in the Divine Light movement, worshiping an Indian adolescent as the bearer of all divine virtue and truth;[20] the chieftain of Toronto's imitative movement, Andy Wernick, reported publicly on the high number of nervous breakdowns among his followers, and so on . . .[21]

During the sixties, irrational motivations among student intellectuals converged with socio-political forces. Some gratified sadistic longings through terrorism; others fulfilled masochistic desires by serving the lowliest in the community; some glorified incest with their mothers by naming their political sect after that act, while others called for the smashing of monogamy; some wanted a totalitarian society in which they would rule as the first among equals, while others in the Movement desired a society of associations and communes; some chose the hippie lifestyle in which they could play all day and transport their egos on voyages borne by hallucinogenic waves of smoke; others wished to cultivate the austere simplicity advocated in Chairman Mao's manual on the conduct of life; some rejected the foods of the "system," and tied their political rebellion to a gastronomical one: convinced that the foodstuffs and water were hopelessly contaminated under the free market system and sensitive as well to the cruelty which sacrificed animals for consumption by man, they became vegetarians.

Vegetarianism flourished on communes of the New Left, while many a "free university" was founded on a curriculum of astrology, magic, and necromancy. *Time* Magazine in 1967 cited the new generation as its "Man of the Year" for its commitment to the fundamental Western ethos, as "a new kind of generation," though the *Nation*, an organ of the Old Left, was troubled by the young's obsession with immediate gratification. The cultural revolution, or "the counterculture," was widely heralded as a prelude to the end of competitive capitalist civilization: "bell-bottoms, workclothes, Army jackets, flowers, beads, guitars, drop-outs, orgies, pot parties, communes, panhandling, underground papers, records, psychedelic posters, buttons."[22]

Seventy years ago Max Weber wrote that the Protestant Ethic had been a necessary condition for the origin and rise of capitalism; the New Left, having been nurtured on introductory sociology courses, drew the corollary: undermine the Protestant Ethic and capitalism will collapse.

This phenomenon might be called the "congelation" or "convergence of neuroses." Whatever one's variety of psychological discontent, whether sadistic or masochistic, authoritarian or anti-authoritarian, ascetic or promiscuous, order-seeking or primitivist, all became vectors added and carried on the same wave to overwhelm the competitive capitalist society.

REJECTION OF TRADITIONAL VALUES

Thus, the socialist sects, groups, factions, and submovements merged into "the Movement" as it became generically known in the sixties.[23] Underlying "the Movement" was a deep-seated revolt against the older generation's mode of life and philosophy, a revolution in what they called "lifestyle" (still another word absorbed from the introductory sociology textbook). To repudiate the values of the elders in 1969 consequently meant to repudiate their capitalist economy, no matter what its record of achievement. Productivity and comfort were rejected as criteria of human progress. A primitivist impulse welled up against the civilization of the schools. "All schools are prisons," wrote Jerry Rubin, echoing the sentiments of Paul

Goodman. But, "the Movement" embraced only one common aim: the abolition of the capitalist system. What then was to supersede it? At this point, all those propounding the diverse psychological modes, all the different types of neuroses and feelings of frustration, all the kinds of political unconscious tried to project on the new social future their particular versions of what might best be called *"post-neurotic society."* The "hedonistic anarchist," as Abbie Hoffman called himself, vaguely visualized a world of multiplied communes; the revived Trotskyites foresaw the advent of a "workers' dictatorship," that is, the benevolent rule of intellectuals; the first "generation" of SDS looked to an alliance with the poor, but the second generation in 1966, having become disenchanted with that idea, frankly saw the university students as both the new historical governing elite and class.[24] Then there were those, especially among the self-anointed Weathermen, who were less interested in the new society than in the satisfactions offered by terrorist activity against the old. They had given up on reading books (their leaders said in 1969 that they had not read a book in a year)[25] and found an immense gratification in the stealth and secrecy of the underground—manufacturing bombs, plotting bombings, clashing with the "pigs," and storming university halls. The catchword of the Weathermen in 1970 was "barbarism," and the Weathermen averred that their role in modern society was similar to that of "the Vandals and Visigoths, who invaded and destroyed the decadent, corrupt Rome."[26] The keynote speaker at their 1969 convention exulted in a cult of personality of the murderer Charles Manson. The next speaker stated more prosaically: "We're against everything that is good and decent."[27]

How, then, can one account for the animus against the market system which grew while books were being written to celebrate the "affluent society"? The aggressive energies of those generations which pioneered and developed modern agriculture and technology were absorbed in a confrontation with problems of the external world. Family rifts were secondary, since aggressive drives were diverted into struggles for livelihood and into mastering the environment. But matters are otherwise when a virtual equilibrium is achieved between the society and its physical environment. When an unprecedented plateau of comfort is attained for a large class of persons, so that there are no basic challenges, there ensues what we might call a *reversal of the polarity of the socio-magnetic field.* The aggressive energies that were previously directed outward in commerce and industry are now turned inward against the self or against society.

It used to be said that man is a problem-solving animal, that he solves problems posed to him by obstacles in the external physical and social environment. The living organism aims at reinstating an equilibrium, as Herbert Spencer said, between the outer and inner relations. John Dewey's whole theory of knowledge is based on the notion that intelligence is an instrument for solving problems posed by disequilibria arising in the external environment. Now this description has certainly been true for the greater part of human history. But, when man seems to have solved his basic problems, he becomes a problem-seeking animal. The excessive, accumulating aggressive energies within him call for external obstacles which do not exist. Or, if obstacles do exist, like those of the problems of space exploration and scientific research, they lie far out of the range of the intellectual powers of most of youth, even children of well-to-do parents. They serve as a challenge only to the most talented fraction.

In the American literature of the late fifties there was a search for a new "purpose," that is, a new problem, to challenge the energies of the young; unfortunately, such a problem was not forthcoming. And so aggressive energies began to turn toward regressive goals. The young who had grown up enjoying the fruits of the capitalist system felt guilty (self-aggressive) with these fruits; they rejected the capitalist way of life, hated its comforts, and exalted those who had not partaken of the fleshpots of material and cultural advances. The new ethic of self-aggression entailed a denigration of material success, of the beauties of art and language, of the structure of law, and of the criteria by which the market allocated places, privileges, and rewards. The "alienation" felt by those whose lives had been so comfortable, so relatively problemless in an external sense as to be near the social-thermodynamic absolute zero, was the recoil of energies expended against oneself and one's family. It was precisely because the free market was so successful that a violently emotional assault was launched against that society.

SUPERIOR INTELLIGENCE AND THE LOSS OF A SENSE OF REALITY

A number of middle-aged psychologists, sympathetic to the New Left, have published studies which depict the young revolutionaries as having been persons from an intellectually superior mold, psychologically healthy, flexible, tolerant, and accepting of their parents' liberal values, which they emulated and extended.[28] The argument for the continuity of the values of the young with those of their elders scarcely jibes with such rather obvious reactions as the activists' revolt against the institution of the monogamous family. Moreover, from 1965 onward, to become an SDS member "meant breaking with your family, it meant being cut off —it was like in early Rome joining a Christian sect . . ."[29] Their leaders were college "drop-outs."

Leftist psychologists have misapprehended the character of the "dialogue" between the young activists and the older generation, especially in those cases in which basic values seemed manifestly shared. For what does it mean "to emulate and extend" the "basic values" that one shares with one's parents? Rigorous "emulation" and "ex-

128

tension" also have been among the classic instruments of generational revolt. For example: a father says that he believes in the equality of all men, meaning equality of opportunity in employment; whereupon the son affirms that he too believes in "equality," but he "extends" the concept to mean equality of condition for all; thereupon the son denounces equality of opportunity as hypocritical and advocates the administration, for instance, of racial quotas in industry and education.[30] Thus, the meaning of "equality" is altered to provide the ethical basis not for a competitive capitalist society, but for a planned one. Obviously, the same word "equality" was used, but the same value "equality" was not shared by its various users. Extending a concept's meaning to the point at which it suppresses a polar value still remains the favored device for grounding a charge of "hypocrisy" against the older generation. This drama was often enacted in the families of the so-called "red-diaper babies," the children of parents who had been communists, or communist oppositionists, or fellow-travelers during an earlier era.[31] Children of communists indeed made it a special point, even when they called themselves communists, to differentiate their standpoint from that of their forebears.

During the thirties, psychological studies were regularly published which purported to show that communist students were the most intelligent and emotionally balanced. These studies had their counterpart in the sixties, though the qualification

129

was sometimes made that leftists' intelligence was superior in verbal though not in mathematical skills.[32] The first samples that psychologists studied in the early sixties had not yet developed overtly violent traits of generational rebellion against their parents' values. A Yale psychiatrist, who admired his early student interviewees, was rebuked later in the decade for his naïveté by one of his Harvard subjects. Young radicals, said the subject, should be skeptical of Dr. Keniston's "lavish praise of his subjects' families," which Dr. Keniston claimed were characterized by "the unusually strong ambivalence of the sons towards fathers whom they often perceived as principled but ineffectual." The subject felt that the leftist psychiatrist had not understood the family relationships of New Leftist children in the upper middle class. The leftist psychiatrist had, moreover, failed to allow for the attraction to drugs and terrorism in his softly limned portrait.[33]

The life stories of the SDS leaders reveal in these types an inability to concentrate upon a subject and a propensity for aimless movement, for striking attitudes of opposition and for dilettantism. Almost no leading activist, furthermore, was a student of the sciences, either physical or mathematical—subjects which demand perseverance and persistence from their students.

Political psychologists have indeed overlooked a basic question in their inquiry into the nature of the leftist intelligence: Can superior intelligence

130

itself make one vulnerable to regressive emotional responses? One researcher concluded after studying several highly gifted people that their "unusual intelligence served to weaken the operation of the reality principle."[34] The gifted person indeed may also be the penalized one; unlike his more plodding fellows, he may have mastered things so quickly that he has not had the need to develop the capacity for postponing gratification; his talents may have given him a feeling of possessing magical powers. His accumulated information and awareness of problems may have outrun the emotional resources of his pre-adolescent and adolescent years. Sensitive, sometimes traumatically so, to his parents' weaknesses long before others, his mind may then have been transfused into a highly emotionalized aggressive instrument. The impact of his insights and empathies may have then made his crisis of development much harder to overcome. In the eyes of classmates and friends, moreover, superior intellectuality smacks of effeminacy. Sometimes young intellectuals, therefore, hide their achievements and interests. Perhaps herein lies another psychological source of the back-to-the-people movements, which in our own time have led intellectuals to revolt against their intellectualism and to adopt the dress of the unskilled laborer. Furthermore, the more intelligent children, losing confidence in their parents at an earlier age, have been observed to experience greater "difficulty in resolving their Oedipus com-

131

plex." And, meanwhile, their "effortless perfection" at school reinforced a feeling of "infantile narcissistic omnipotence."

THE HUMANISTIC INTELLECTUALS

Fortunate are the talented ones whose interests and activities are channeled into the physical and natural sciences or into engineering, all of which provide the healthy experience of working with physical reality. The literary or humanistic intellectual, by contrast, lacks the ballast of empirical verification for his hypotheses, often conceived as emotional responses. If he empathizes with the sufferings of men under the yoke of the market system, he forthwith visualizes a social system in which these sufferings will be removed. His logical, aesthetic, and imaginative powers are, however, at the behest of his emotional will-to-believe. It is difficult for him to ask detachedly: What are the advantages and disadvantages of different social systems? How do different types of human character respond under varied social conditions? How frustrating, satisfying, and conducive to creativity are different social systems? Which systems restrict personal freedoms most? These questions may seem secondary, pettifogging, and obstructive from the standpoint of the warmhearted, humanistic intellectual. Reason is then the servant of rationalization rather than of scientific investigation. The humanistic intellectual's superior mind may do superior violence to the facts,

132

like the child who uses his intelligence to destroy a resisting toy.

Thus, those communist students who, according to Columbia and City College psychiatrists, possessed superior intelligence often were those who swallowed the validity of the Moscow trials, Stalin's version of history, and the pact between Stalin and Hitler. The editors of *The New Republic*—able, civic-minded, and gifted writers—likewise endorsed the judgments of the Moscow trials. Men of ideas, Max Lerner once wrote, want to toughen themselves in order to convert their ideas into weapons. The "hard" scientist, the engineer, or the technologist sublimates his generational aggression by coping with the environment. The humanistic intellectual, on the other hand, oscillates between fantasy and force. Only the strongest factual refutation, or the disappearance, or obsolescence through age, of his impulse to generational revolt will disenthrall his mind. The language of "the god that failed" is that of humanistic intellectuals stirred by nonrational motives to fashion gods for themselves. Their theorizing on the alternatives to the capitalist system is often akin to a quest in political theology. Rarely does a scientist whose hypothesis is disproved think of it as a god that failed.

The unprecedented rise in the number of humanistic intellectuals in recent times disproportionately increased the number of "dialectical personalities" within the intellectual elite. Hence, the compulsion to assail the capitalist market system spread. Whenever a problem arose, the solution offered was socialism. And, because socialism was the only alternative to capitalism ever mentioned, the intellectuals felt that it had the mandate of "historical inevitability." A thoroughgoing "dialectical" generational revolt against the competitive capitalist system meant "negating" it and affirming socialism, its polar opposite.

SOCIALISM IN THE UNIVERSITIES

In his great book *Capitalism, Socialism, and Democracy,* Joseph Schumpeter argued that the over-expansion of universities multiplies the number of those "psychically unemployable in lower occupations" and nurtures "a discontented frame of mind." When the New Left emerged in the 1960s, the university intellectuals and students were indeed enjoying the best economic prospects ever; professorships, grants, and research fellowships were plentiful. Professors were the most respected group among the President's Cabinet and advisors. Thus, the economics of unemployment was not the prime mover of their socialist yearning and their conviction that the free market was the breeding ground of alienation. Schumpeter advances along with his economic explanation a more psychological-institutional one. He refers to "the intellectual spectator's typical attitude toward men, classes, and civilizations."

Many a sociologist or political scientist has felt unfulfilled in the academy, for his true vocation, he feels, is to change society. No doubt he has repeated to himself the aphorism of Marx: "The philosophers have only interpreted the world; the point, however, is to change it."

The only great engineer who also was a socialist was Charles P. Steinmetz. In his case, the socialist aspiration arose from the tragedy of his misshapen body. He would tell his General Electric colleagues and Schenectady fellow-citizens that he wanted a world in which all children would be "symmetrical." And his socialist faith was conceived in a Bismarckian Germany, where Jewish descent still disenfranchised one in the universities and where socialists were persecuted.[35]

Likewise, the socialism of Oppenheimer and Einstein was far more a response to the persecution of their fellow Jews than it was to any dissatisfaction with capitalism. No doubt Disraeli was right when he said that it was the specific circumstance of such persecution or its memory which turned young Jews into revolutionaries. But anti-Semitism is an artificial restriction on the competitive capitalist market, not something which is part of it. The decline of anti-Semitism first began in the free market society of the Dutch commercial towns in the sixteenth and seventeenth centuries.

Scientists and inventors usually have perceived that their work fared better in an environment predominantly competitive and capitalist than in a planned economy. The courageous Soviet physicist Andrei Sakharov recently enunciated:

135

It is no accident that for many years, in our country, new and promising scientific trends in biology and cybernetics could not develop normally, while on the surface out-and-out demagogy, ignorance, and charlatanism bloomed like gorgeous flowers. It is no accident that all the great scientific and technological discoveries of recent times—quantum mechanics, new elementary particles, uranium fission, antibiotics, and most of the new, highly effective drugs, transistors, electronic computers, the discovery of other components of the "Green Revolution," and the creation of new technologies in agriculture, industry, and construction—all of them happened outside our country.[36]

The humanistic intellectuals are the ones who basically shape the ethos of the universities. In previous years a very high percentage of students used to "work their way" through college. This experience had an important value; it reinforced contact with reality and provided a counterweight against tendencies to social fantasy. The Marxist or Marcusean phrases about work and workingmen ring hollow to those who have worked side by side with them. But the students, now a highly favored stratum, are liberally subsidized and their experience is much more wholly university-centered. Thus, the paradox: at the very time when university students call for a greater involvement with society, they are more isolated from it in an everyday, workaday sense than they ever have been in the United States. Together with the direction of

136

their generational revolt, university culture reinforces the anti-capitalist mentality.[37]

GUILT FEELINGS AND EGALITARIANISM

It would be wrong, however, to think of "university socialism" as founded solely on the ingredient of power-striving. It is fed as well by a strong sense of justice tied to a sense of guilt.[38] Such a sense of justice was the strongest motive in making a socialist, for example, of R. H. Tawney, the distinguished economic historian. So profound was his rebellion against his family's commercial achievements that he showed no interest in its annals. Influenced by Ruskin, Morris, and the Christian tradition, he felt guilty about the wealth he enjoyed but which was denied to most men. Like the Russian students who went "back to the people," Tawney went into the Workers' Educational Association. The experience of what he called "the spirit of comradeship" made him a socialist. It had little to do with theoretical analysis, for Tawney had a "lifelong disesteem for theoretical economics," and wrote in his diary that there was no such science.[39] When he joined the British Army, in the First World War, he insisted on remaining in the ranks as an enlisted man.

People experience a sense of justice in two ways. One sense, as Russell noted, is "rationalized envy"; the man who is denied opportunities given to others and who regards himself as equally qualified feels resentful. In the second case, a sense of justice

137

reflects a feeling of guilt experienced by those who are privileged; it is often associated with strong masochistic feelings and a tendency toward self-destruction or civilization-destruction. Tawney, in his ascetic mood, felt that if a society could be just only if it were poor, then poverty should be decreed.[40] Shaw, the egalitarian, was ready to have the human race consigned to extinction by the Life Force for its failure to realize his socialist vision. Yet, if Neanderthal men had been egalitarians or if a masochistic sense of justice had prevailed in their ideology, would there have been evolutionary progress?

The egalitarian animus against the free market is rooted deeply in certain infantile and childhood experiences. The child's entry into a competitive society has, as we have seen, a traumatic ingredient. The child's earliest society consists primarily of his mother, and then of his family. In a sense, a maternalistic society made up of the mother and the child is the primordial one. The father, who disappears daily into the unknown world of "work," will one day induct the child into the competitive society. The child begins to play games in which other children win and perceives that the advantage goes to the strong, the wily, the cunning. The child may come to dislike "winning games" and prefer to play games where everyone "takes turns." The imagery of ethical communism always calls to mind these early childhood memories of the primal social organization, the family, and the trauma of competition. It also evokes the longing to return to the society in which we once were as a family, all brothers and sisters. Marx, to be sure, later hated such slogans as "All men are brothers," because he wanted a movement based on struggle. Psychologically, though, Marx's earlier use of the world "alienation" had articulated the longing to return to the precompetitive primordial society.

Today's younger generation probably has enjoyed more maternal care and affection than any previous one. Families have become smaller and mothers have been barraged with so vast an amount of literature on child care that the actual attention received by the average child may have reached its highest level. For many, then, the encounter with the competitive society has probably been all the more traumatic. To "lose" in a game awakens unconscious fears that one is no longer loved, that, above all, the hostile father will reject one. The "born loser" internalizes this fear of defeat, of rejection by others, and rejects the competitive society, the "rat race," before it can reject him. In a more maternal, socialist society, he avers, he would receive his just recognition. Thus, the intense hostility to the free market of the 1960s.

THE APPEAL OF THE PLANNED ECONOMY; THE COLLECTIVIZATION OF THE MIND

As more educational opportunities have become available, with a college education accessible to virtually all, it is more difficult to blame the "system" for one's failure. In the days when only the upper class was educated, there were many persons who could feel (as the protagonist in Hardy's *Jude the Obscure* felt) that they were not given the chance to realize their scholarly potentialities. But nearly everyone now gets that chance. Those who fail today tend, therefore, to regard equal educational opportunity as part of the "rat race" which impoverishes one's personality and stifles creativity. The growing number of discontented quasi-scholars project images of their social transfiguration on the "system's" polar alternative, the planned socialist economy. If the free market is the stage of one's defeat, then let the theater be changed.

Thus, although men of superior intelligence have sought to replace the free market with socialism they have invariably been displaced as society's rulers by the mediocrats, men with inordinate political ambition but mediocre intelligence. Socialist society tends to evolve into a mediocracy, where the Platonic philosopher-guardians are replaced by ideological guards.

Mediocrities have indeed perceived that a planned economy enables them to satisfy certain aggressive drives and longings. Though a poet such as Voznesensky, a novelist such as Solzhenitsyn, a scientist such as Sakharov, have attained prominence in a planned socialist order, the power-seeking mediocrities can always vent their jealousy against such men of genius by threatening and humiliating them, or worse: Mandelstam was killed; Solzhenitsyn exiled; Sakharov deprived of teaching and research positions. In our society, a great uprising of the mediocracy against the meritocracy has been taking place. Many thousands of mediocre students, "non-students," and "dropouts" resent the emphasis on achievement and excellence and the high order of ability demonstrated by the scientists who advance our knowledge of the world and explore space. The so-called underground journals in 1969 engaged in a bitter outburst when the first landing on the moon took place. They expressed the jealousy of mediocrities who, unable "to make history," decide that they can unmake history by disruption.

Communist organization is, above all, the instrument of the mediocrats. The Communist Party, notes one of its former leading political analysts, "attracted the insecure, the rebellious, the lonely, or the authoritarian personalities"; the functionaries who dominated the party apparatus were no "mass figures" but anonymous mediocrities.[41]

The more talented the person, the more the Communist Party feared he might perceive and expose the shallowness of the pronouncements made by the mediocrities in power. Factions were expelled from the party because their chief personalities were men of far greater ability than those of the official party organization. Among the Trotskyite intellectuals in the United States were such writers as Max Eastman, Mary McCarthy, Dwight Macdonald; the "right deviationist Love-

141

stoneites" included such able scholars and thinkers as Bertram Wolfe and Will Herberg; and among the philosophers outside the Communist fold was Sidney Hook. The official party organs of literature and the social sciences were by contrast composed of stale, unoriginal minds. Any man with an original mind was weeded out by the Politburo as a likely "deviationist." The Politburo was usually correct in its suspicion. Thus, the "splits" always involved a winnowing out of those with the highest intelligence. The inferiocrats struggled for hegemony over the superiocrats.[42]

Even the plodding Theodore Dreiser was carefully excluded by the Communists as unreliable until he was old and subdued. The mediocrities, jealous and envious, enjoyed using their bureaucratic power to compensate for their incompetence. As an editor of *New Masses* recollects, "Not a few have asked themselves: if they were capable of such cruelties to each other when they were a small handful of people bound by sacred ideals, what might they have done if they had been in power?"[43]

COMMUNISM AS MEDIOCRACY

Where Communists rule, as in the Soviet Union, mediocrities have access to power and influence. The early Bolsheviks included such superior men as Lenin and Bukharin and were joined by the intellectual aristocrat Trotsky. It was the mediocrities, however, represented by Stalin, and the gov-

142

ernmental and bureaucratic personnel, who made up the backbone of the party. The ablest of the Soviet sociologists, Andrei Amalrik, has written:

> The systematic removal from the life of society of the most independent and most active of its members, which has been going on for decades, has left an imprint of greyness and mediocrity on all sections of society—and this could not fail to be reflected in the "middle class" which is once again taking shape.
>
> In the mass this group is so mediocre, its thinking is so "bureaucratized" and the section of it which is intellectually most independent is so passive . . .

He also writes: "In practice, 'justice' is motivated by the wish "nobody should be better off than me.' This idea is motivated by hatred for everything that is outstanding."[44] The party-state monopoly in every walk of life, writes Sakharov, "demands that people become hypocrites, timeservers, mediocre . . ."[45]

Social structure may shape character, but in a more fundamental sense, character determines social structure. The party hack relishes the opportunity that a planned socialist system provides to humiliate those whose abilities provoke his jealousy. The poet Andrei Voznesensky was bullied by the editor-in-chief of *Pravda,* who threatened that "he would be ground to dust" if he didn't connive at official lies.[46] When the famed geneticist Nikolai Vavilov was interrogated a hundred times during the course of eleven months and his spirit was

143

broken to prepare for his body's death in a labor camp, it was an envious, unsuccessful assistant, Shudenko, who directed the investigation. Upwardly mobile, mediocre graduate students found their mediocrity valued by the state as they led the denunciation of abler men. The way was opened, writes the Soviet historian-biologist Zhores Medvedev, "for a large number of people incapable of real and serious creative work . . . and with a personal interest in continued persecution of genetics and biology to receive scientific degrees and positions."[47]

In the field of physics, an ignorant, envious party officialdom, abetted by a "jury" of machine-shop workers, penalized such brilliant graduate students as Lev Landau and George Gamow for accepting Einstein's theory of relativity.[48] And this mediocratic hostility would have persisted in the Soviet Union, had it not been for the power of the continuing free market for ideas in the international realm. When the United States developed atomic energy, the Soviet bureaucrats had to swallow their dislike for the theory of relativity and allow their physicists to go their own way. But what would have been the fate of scientific freedom had the international free market for ideas been destroyed? The scientists would then have fared as Aleksandr Solzhenitsyn did with the Moscow Writers' Union, whose literary bureaucrats vetoed the publication of his novels, enveloped him with a barrage of propagandist lies, and mourned the good old Stalinist days when they

144

simply would have had him condemned to the labor camp, the dungeon, or death. Even as the Soviet regime achieved a "collectivization of agriculture" by destroying the free market in farm products and "liquidating" the better farmers, that is, the "kulaks," they likewise, in the intellectual domain, have carried out what might best be called the "collectivization of the mind." In practice, this collectivization signified the hegemony of the mediocrats in every intellectual field. At the universities, as Solzhenitsyn writes, if a student denounced a lecturer for not citing Stalin, that was "all that was needed for the lecturer not to show up for lectures any more."[49]

Shortly after Stalin's death, a Soviet critic, V. Pomerantsev, dared to describe the "collective" pressures exerted by the Writers' Union and the publishing houses, which made for insincerity. He said, "I have heard that Shakespeare wasn't a member of a union at all, yet he did not write badly." One can imagine what a committee of mediocrats, dedicated to socialist realism or its bourgeois counterpart in Elizabethan times, would have done with Hamlet's soliloquy. "Comrade Shakespeare," they would have said, "this is much too negative, too pessimistic. You do not show the positive role of the emerging bourgeoisie, which is developing the forces of production and will conquer feudal pessimism. To be concerned with the afterlife is metaphysical idealism, which will be overcome by the new commercial and industrial expansion. 'To take arms against a sea of troubles' should be re-written as a call to revolution and the question is not 'to be or not to be,' but rather 'to be alienated and estranged from the masses or to be identified with them'; no more of this proto-bourgeois individualism."

It is one of the curious facts of intellectual history that such men as Marx and Shaw placed themselves with the movement for collectivization, for neither man could have abided any attempt to interfere with his freedom. Marx avoided meetings and demonstrations and took pride in his isolated position outside any party; Shaw went off to Ayot St. Lawrence, his rural retreat. Marx may have advocated the communal life of cooperative association, but he probably wouldn't have lasted more than a week in any one of them—an Israeli kibbutz, or a Yugoslav or Chinese commune. He knew the joys of alienated life in a competitive capitalist society, not the least of which is the freedom to rail against it, and all such joys would have been denied him under communism.

FOOTNOTES

1. William Morris, *Selected Writings and Designs,* Asa Briggs, ed. (Harmondsworth: Penguin, 1962), pp. 149, 150.

2. *Ibid.,* p. 149.

3. Erich Fromm, *The Sane Society* (New York: Fawcett Reprint, 1955), p. 111.

4. *Current Biography* (New York: H. W. Wilson, 1969), p. 282.

5. Bernard Landes and Edward S. Tauber, eds., *In the Name of Life: Essays in Honor of Erich Fromm* (New York: Holt, Rinehart & Winston, 1971), p. x.

6. Karl Marx and Friedrich Engels, *Correspondence 1846–1895,* Dona Torr, trans. (New York: International Publications, 1935), p. 91.

7. Bernard Shaw, *Everybody's Political What's What* (London: Constable and Company., 1945), pp. 283–5.

8. Thorsten Veblen, *Essays in our Changing Order,* Leon Ardzrooni, ed. (New York: Viking Press, 1934), pp. 439–44.

9. *Ibid.,* p. 403.

10. Herbert Marcuse, "Ecology and Revolution," *Liberation,* Vol. 17, No. 6, Sept. 1972, pp. 10–12.

11. *Pravda,* June 26, 1970. Cited in John M. Kramer, "Environmental Problems in the USSR: The Divergence of Theory and Practice," *The Journal of Politics,* Vol. 36 (1974), p. 890. "Managers know that so long as they fulfill plan targets their grateful ministries will not complain . . ." *Ibid.,* p. 891.

12. The distinguished psychiatrist Helene Deutsch knew and observed the two outstanding women of the pre–World War I socialist movement, Rosa Luxemburg and Angelica Balabanoff. She noted how Rosa had "transferred her adolescent rebellion from her family to the whole of bourgeois society;" Rosa might have been "a good subject for a psycho-analytical biography," she added. Angelica too "began her rebellion inside the family"; her hatred of her aristocratic mother was so strong as to lead her in her youth "to a life of self-imposed poverty and suffering." *Confrontations With Myself* (New

147

York: Norton, 1973), pp. 98, 101. Dr. Deutsch's own political activism stemmed too, she writes, from a "vigorous adolescent rebellion" against her parents; hating her mother, she had a "dangerous love" for her father. *Ibid.*, pp. 80, 85.

13. Erich Fromm, *The Sane Society,* reprinted (New York: Fawcett, 1955), p. 108.

14. Karl Marx, *Capital,* p. 148. *Economic and Philosophical Manuscripts of 1844,* Martin Milligan, trans. (Moscow: Foreign Languages Publishing House, 1961), p. 137.

15. Fromm, *op. cit.,* p. 120.

16. " 'Mario and I, who had both fought the University of California, flipped out at the same time and wound up committed inside the system,' Mr. Schmorleitz said." *The New York Times,* Oct. 12, 1974.

17. Lewis S. Feuer, "Student Unrest in the United States," *The Annals of the American Academy of Political and Social Science,* Vol. 404 (Nov. 1972), pp. 171–3.

18. *Loc. cit.* Dotson Rader reports that he has counted seventeen suicides among his fellow activists. "Firing Line," Public Television Station WNET, N.Y., April 24, 1976.

19. *The Varsity,* Toronto, January 7, 1976. "Before psychic therapy and EST, I didn't know where my parents ended and I began . . . As I grow older, I get closer and closer to the little boy in me . . . We competed for attention like media junkies after a fix . . . We always have to fight the self-destructive urge within ourselves. Abbie, who knows what incredible internal psychic factors have driven you underground?" Jerry Rubin, "To Abbie Hoffman, Wherever He's Hiding Out," *The New York Times,* January 24, 1976. Also, *The New York Times,* February 11, 1976.

20. *The New York Times,* May 5, 1973. Michael Rossman, "Bliss and Fear in Berkeley," *Social Policy,* Sept.–Oct. 1974, Vol. 5, No. 3, pp. 33–7. Andrew Kopkind, "Mystic Politics:

Refugees from the New Left," *Ramparts,* Vol. 12, July 1973, p. 50.

21. " 'I keep in touch with the left,' he says . . . 'There was a lot of nervous breakdowns then. A lot.' " Hartley Steward, "The Quiet Campus," *The Toronto Star,* May 12, 1973.

22. Kirkpatrick Sale, *SDS* (New York: Random House, 1973), pp. 345, 349.

23. *Ibid.,* p. 7.

24. Sale, *op. cit.,* p. 292.

25. *Ibid.,* p. 580.

26. John Kifner, "Vandals in the Mother Country," *The New York Times Magazine,* January 4, 1970, p. 15 ff.

27. Bernardine Dohrn, secretary for SDS in 1968–69, said that Weathermen "dig" Manson because he was "badly" incestuous in an Oedipal fashion, and also because of the brutality of his murders: "Dig it, first they killed those pigs, then they ate dinner in the same room with them, then they even shoved a fork into a victim's stomach! Wild!" *The Militant,* January 16, 1970, p. 12. *The New York Times,* March 11, 1970.

28. Sale, *op. cit.,* p. 350.

29. *Ibid.,* p. 206. A typical "yippie" leaflet which circulated in Chicago in 1968 at the time of the demonstrations against the Democratic National Convention and which was commended by Tom Hayden, SDS president and later one of the "Chicago Seven," for its "beautiful sentiments" sounded the tocsin of generational revolt: "disobey your parents. Burn your money. You know life is a dream, and all our institutions are manmade illusions, effective because you take the cream for reality. Break down the family, church, nature, city, economy, turn life into an art form. . . . The revolutionary is only an artist. What is needed is a generation of people who are freaky, crazy, irrational, sexy, angry, irreligious, childish, and

mad. People who burn draft cards, burn high school, and college degrees, people who say 'to hell with your goals!' People who lure the youth with music, pot, and acid, people who redefine the normal, people who break with the status-royal-title-consumer game, people who . . . have more in common with Indians plundered than they do with their own parents. Burn your houses down, and you will be free." Tom Hayden, *Rebellion and Regression:* Testimony by Tom Hayden before the National Commission on the Causes and Prevention of Violence, and the House Un-American Activities Committee (New York: World Publishing Co., 1969), p. 186.

30. The phrase "equality of condition" was evidently first used by the aesthetic socialist William Morris. Cf. William Morris, *op. cit.,* p. 33.

31. Sale, *op.cit.,* pp. 88–9, 468.

32. Sale, *op. cit.,* p. 350.

33. Nicholas Basingstoke, "Is the New Left Really *That* Good? *The Young Radicals,* by Kenneth Keniston," *Liberation,* May 1, 1969, pp. 32–4. Martin Duberman, "Youth and Dissent," *N.Y. Times Book Review,* April 2, 1972, p. 4.

34. Sylvan Keiser, "Superior Intelligence: Its Contribution to Neurogenesis," *Journal of the American Psychoanalytic Association,* Vol. 17, 1969, pp. 452–73.

35. John Winthrop Hammond, *Charles Proteus Steinmetz* (New York: Center, 1924), p. 71 ff. James Burkhardt Gilbert, *Designing the Industrial State: The Intellectual Pursuit of Collectivism in America, 1880–1940* (Chicago: Quadrangle Books, 1972), p. 194.

36. Andrei D. Sakharov, *My Country and the World,* trans., Guy V. Daniels (New York: Random House, Vintage ed., 1975), p. 31.

37. Recently, in the 1974 academic term, a Canadian consulting firm undertook a survey of university students' attitudes

toward business. They conducted interviews with more than a thousand students on eight Ontario campuses. They found indeed a widespread anti-capitalist mentality: 77 percent of the students had a negative opinion of the overall performance of the Canadian business community; 86 percent felt the profit motive had done more harm than good to society; 85 percent rejected the traditional role and values of the work ethic in society; 62 percent had become more negative toward business during the previous two years. "Business: Phoenix or Fossil," *Like It Is,* Vol. 1, No. 4, 1975, p. 23.

38. The austere Marxist communism, for instance, was "strong in the Boston area" and "always well represented in the Harvard/Radcliffe chapters" because (it was alleged) "only the sons and daughters of the aristocracy have sufficient guilt to join disciplined parties laboring on behalf of the working masses . . ." Sale, *op. cit.,* p. 539.

39. Ross Terrill, *R. H. Tawney and His Times: Socialism as Fellowship* (Cambridge, Mass.: Harvard University Press, 1973), pp. 22, 36–7.

40. J. M. Winter, *Socialism and the Challenge of War* (London: Routledge and Kegan Paul, 1974), p. 86.

41. Joseph Starobin, *American Communism in Crisis, 1943–57* (Cambridge, Mass.: Harvard University Press, 1972), pp. 234, 40.

42. Nathan Glazer has argued that "any one of a dozen little accidents, such as who one's friends or uncle were, who ran the best social affairs, which groups were nearby, might turn one young man into a Socialist, another into a Communist, a third into a Lovestoneite." Cf. *The Social Basis of American Communism* (New York: Harcourt Brace, 1961), p. 40. Actually, character and intelligence were the most important determinants. The Lovestoneites had the strongest political bent, their intellectuals making up mostly a latter World War I group; the Trotskyites included the most brilliant literary intellectuals of the pre-Depression and early Depression era.

151

The Communists with their disciplined orthodoxy and promise of victory had the highest percentage of mediocrities. Although the nonacademic intellectuals were drawn to the Trotskyites, the academic ones, however, tended to fall into the Stalinist orbit, either as Communists or as fellow-travelers. At Harvard University in the late thirties, this was especially true; David Prall, F. O. Matthiessen, and Paul M. Sweezy were the most well-known examples, but there were notably no Trotskyites. At Columbia University, where there were Jewish Marxists with a long political tradition, some experienced Trotskyites affected the political environment. At City College, however, in 1939 there was a large section of Communists, mostly Jews, but no Trotskyites; compared to the Trotskyites, they were younger and rather pedestrian in their abilities, and often owed their posts to the rapid expansion of the city colleges during the Depression.

43. Starobin, *op. cit.*, p. 199.

44. Andrei Amalrik, "Will the U.S.S.R. Survive Until 1984?" *Survey,* No. 73, Autumn 1969, pp. 54–6, 62–3.

45. Sakharov, *op. cit.*, p. 30.

46. *Problems of Communism,* Vol. XVII (Sept.–Oct. 1968), p. 48.

47. Zhores Aleksandrovich Medvedev, *The Rise and Fall of T. D. Lysenko,* trans., I. Michael Lerner (New York: Columbia University Press, 1969), p. 142. Also cf. pp. 56, 129.

48. George Gamow, *My World Line: An Informal Autobiography* (New York: Viking Press, 1970), pp. 93–9, 120.

49. Aleksandr I. Solzhenitsyn, *The Gulag Archipelago,* trans., Thomas P. Whitney, Vol. I–II (New York: Harper and Row, 1974), paperback ed., p. 73.

6

A Comment on "Some Irrational Sources of Opposition to the Market System"

Dale Vree

It is an unusual pleasure for me to reply to Lewis Feuer's paper. I feel I have haunted Professor Feuer these many years, just as he has haunted me.

I don't think it is any secret that one of the most dramatic events in Professor Feuer's life was the Free Speech Movement at Berkeley in 1964. That phenomenon clearly aroused great passions on his part and was an "inspiration"—if I may use that term—for much of the extraordinary scholarship he has engaged in over the last several years.

Certainly, the Free Speech Movement (FSM) was also one of the most dramatic events in my life. As in the case of Professor Feuer, I experienced the FSM firsthand. But whereas he was a critic and staunch opponent of the FSM, I was an enthusiastic participant—indeed, I was one of the 800 or so people arrested for taking

153

over Sproul Hall. At that time, it was our impression that Professor Feuer hated us deeply (although I don't know for a fact that such was the case), and we, for our part, certainly hated him in return—not only as a reciprocative gesture, but especially because he was once a radical and therefore a renegade to us.

I have no reason to believe that Professor Feuer has substantially changed his opinions of us in subsequent years. Conversely, I have no reason to believe that those loyal to the FSM legacy have substantially changed their opinions of him. But I, for one, *have* changed my opinion of the FSM, to the point that I am now probably as critical of it as Professor Feuer, if not for all the same reasons.[1]

Willy-nilly, I came to change my opinions of Professor Feuer too. It is because I now have a healthy respect for Professor Feuer's views that I am delighted to have this occasion to comment on his remarks.

My reactions to Professor Feuer's paper will be of two sorts: 1) I shall offer myself—to be precise, my self of circa 1964–5—as a specimen of one who, as a so-called "student revolutionary," passionately hated the market system; 2) I shall comment from the perspective of one who is concerned with the character of Professor Feuer's truth claims.

Feuer begins his paper by dichotomizing human nature in terms of affectional and aggressive drives. He says that

> the most widespread critiques of the free market society, though claiming to be founded on a desire to satisfy repressed affectional longings, often proceed from other drives, even crypto-aggressive ones. The socialist reformer may be concerned less with socialism than with projecting aggressive impulses into a struggle against the market system.

Or, says Professor Feuer, he may hope to play a role in dictatorship, with its secret police, to administer punishments especially against the intellectually independent and superior, or to engage in economic planning because he enjoys in anticipation or vicariously the role of allocating human resources. I suspect that Feuer is largely right here. At least he is right about me (although I am not quite ready to admit to having been an inferior intellectual bent upon punishing my superiors). I was neither a touchie-feelie utopian, a naïve pacifist, nor an incipient hippie. As a Marxist-Leninist, I was quite aware that post-capitalist society would be characterized by dictatorship, secret police, censorship, a command economy, and the like. Indeed, I characterized myself as something of a "neo-Stalinist." Outside of the tragedy of the Great Purges and other needless persecutions, I was entirely at peace with the legacy of Stalinism and with the prospect of what it might entail for the future. This is not to say that I was indifferent to the "affectional" attractions of communist society; rather, I was quite aware of the harsh, "aggressive" measures that would have to be taken in

155

order to reach communism. I would go so far as to say that I consciously practiced verbal deception when propagandizing for the communist cause—that is, I would condemn capitalism for being insufficiently "affectional," insufficiently libertarian, all the while recognizing that a socialist dictatorship would be far less "affectional," far less libertarian, than the capitalism I was condemning. I think I was aware that the "aggressive" aspects of socialism were more immediately attractive to me than the more theoretical "affectional" ones. I had visited the Soviet Union, Poland, Czechoslovakia, and East Germany in the summer of 1964. What had appealed to me most about those societies was not the evidences of brotherhood, goodwill, cooperative endeavor, creativity—much less the supposed material blessings of a socialized economy—but rather the *quality* of life, by which I mean the austerity, the seriousness, the regimentation, the ascetic spirit, and the sense of purpose, struggle, and militance.

In 1966, I had a chance to return to East Germany—this time for four-and-a-half months. During those months I became disillusioned—but not for the usual reasons. That socialist Germany was not as "affectional" as I had expected was a minor irritant. I felt then—and I still feel—that the pace and style of life in East Germany is in many ways more attractive than life in, say, West Germany. Life in the East is probably more "affectional" in general—it is slower, less complicated, less frenzied. That the East German regime was not as "affectional" toward dissenters as West Germany was did not bother me greatly. What really irritated me, however, was that East Germany seemed to be going "bourgeois"—by which I mean going "soft." The struggle for socialism did not *animate* the people (which is really not too surprising), but what was really surprising was that it didn't animate many Party members either. Everybody was interested in material goods, private pursuits, and the "good life." The international struggle for socialism was of much less interest. If I may employ Feuer's terminology, the people were not "projecting" their "aggressive impulses." In a sense, then, life there was *too* "affectional" to suit me.

Having said this, I trust it will be understood when I say I am a bit puzzled by Feuer's statement that "an irrational source of objection to the free market, then, is one which is founded on largely repressed or unconscious feelings, which contravene the person's basic conscious values." Quite the contrary, I think that my feelings at the time *were* avowed, and were *not* "largely repressed or unconscious" (which, of course, says nothing about other people's motivations).

RATIONAL HOSTILITY TO THE MARKET

Feuer says that an example of "rational" opposition to the free market would be that of the "unemployed worker in 1932." That, of course, is a pretty hard act to follow. I cannot, therefore, say that my opposition to the free market was "rational" in a sense which Feuer would allow. On the other hand, my opposition wasn't "irrational" either, at least in Feuer's sense. My opposition was not articulated through the concept of "alienation." To be sure, I had read the young Marx, Erich Fromm, and Herbert Marcuse when I was an undergraduate, but I must say that the concept of alienation never really grabbed me. Although I was a student in the "multiversity," I never felt "alienated" in that environment. I never felt estranged from technology or from industrial, bureaucratic society. I never felt a cosmic sense of normlessness or directionlessness. The atom bomb did not traumatize me. Indeed, if I felt alienated at all, it was from the incessant chatter about alienation on the part of my fellow students. I was angered that students seemed much more interested in sex perversions, obscenity, drugs, and music than in the emancipation of the working class. It seemed to me that their primary concerns—self-gratification, self-expression, and release from personal psychological anxieties—were entirely selfish. The student movement seemed to be more of a mirror image than a viable alternative to the surrounding society. Frankly, it was largely because of the ridiculous posturing and apparent pathology of the student movement that my wife and I decided to flee to East Germany.

Feuer says that the contemporary critics of the free market who moan about alienation are possessed of "dialectical personalities." I'm not sure

whether or not my personality would have qualified, for the dialectical personality invariably has
"a strong ingredient of sadism, in a curiously oscillating relationship with a sacrificial component." I
would certainly resist characterizing my personality of over ten years ago as "sadistic." But Feuer
also says that the dialectical personality is "moved
by a compulsive spirit of contrariety." I wouldn't
want to consider myself a "compulsive" anything,
but I would accept the tag "contrary" or "independent."

If, for the sake of argument, I can admit to having had a "dialectical personality," I am puzzled
by Feuer's claim entailing unconscious feelings of
resentment against one's father, which feelings
are, in turn, projected onto a struggle against the
market system. Here, of course, we have the familiar Oedipal theme, for which Feuer has become
famous.

Why, I wonder, didn't I resent my father? Was
there something wrong with me? It fills me with
some embarrassment to admit that I always loved
and appreciated my father very much. Actually, it
was the positive influence of my father, more than
anything else, which turned me against the market system. My father, the son of an immigrant
mechanic and sheet-metal pressman, instilled in
me an appreciation for the common man, his culture and his trade unions, and a hostility to the "big
boys"—that is, the rich and powerful. The influence had nothing to do with intellectuality. My
father, who did not go to college, did not even

graduate from a normal high school, but finished his schooling at a trade school. He never read Marx and never knew the first thing about Marxism or any other esoteric doctrine. I am sure that he never heard of Herbert Marcuse or Erich Fromm.

Feuer says that the "key elements" in the dialectical personality's indictment of the market system are a hostility to numbers, arithmetic, and quantification—a hostility characteristic of "literary intellectuals." Obviously, my father was no literary intellectual. Indeed, he always had a knack for numbers and employed them constantly in his work as a draftsman. As for myself, I was never hostile to numbers. My aptitude tests always showed a greater facility with things mathematical than with things literary.

If there were any "literary intellectuals" in my family, the only possible candidate would be my mother—the daughter of a housepainter and wallpaper hanger—who, through hard work and determination, became a music teacher in a community college in Southern California. But I certainly never picked up any hostility to the market system from her. She has never uttered a word against the "big boys," much less the capitalist system.

ALIENATION AND STUDENT RADICALISM

I would agree with Feuer that student hostility to the market system in the 1960s focused on a putative experience of "alienation," rather than an experience of exploitation or economic injustice. That was painfully evident to me at the time.

Over the years I have reflected deeply on why I could not relate to my allegedly alienated peers —indeed, why I felt a special loathing for them. The conclusion I have tentatively come to is that my fellow students had markedly different family experiences. Most of them apparently had little anchoring in or affinity for the life experiences of common people. Most of them, I gather, had permissive upbringings and were accustomed to "instant personal gratification." My upbringing was not very permissive, nor did I have much difficulty learning to defer personal gratification. The obstacles and headaches which were to be experienced in the university and industrial society at large struck me as being normal and predictable, whereas my peers seemed to regard them as intolerable.

It is my impression that most of my peers were brought up in upper middle class homes where liberal political values, rooted in the imperative to be tolerant, were taught. In my home, those values were *not* taught. The only political value which I learned was what might be called *ressentiment*— hostility to privileged elites—which I picked up from my father. I was *not* taught the values which my peers apparently picked up in their homes— namely, a concern for world peace, a compassion for racial minorities, a respect for the civil liberties of dissenters and deviants. And, although I learned to hate the decadence and privileges of the rich,

161

I was never taught to abhor competition, money, mathematics, and so on. I was not even taught to hate capitalism. *That* I picked up on my own, as a kind of inference or logical extension of my antipathy to the rich. But the benchmarks in my anticapitalist development were not the writings of Fromm, Marcuse, and Paul Goodman. I was introduced to socialism via the publications of the Socialist and Socialist Labor parties, although the most decisive influence on my thinking was Paul Sweezy's independent Marxist magazine, *Monthly Review.* All these influences, it will be noted, were "Old Left."

Even though I am not prepared to say that Feuer's emphasis on the Oedipus complex and the "generation gap" is fallacious, it does not help me understand my own experiences. My father had a moderate "trade unionist" mentality, whereas I became a revolutionary communist. To Feuer that proves that I was in rebellion against my father. To be sure, I was not a carbon copy of my father. Nevertheless I *understood myself* to be acting out of loyalty to the values of my father. I saw my actions as being congruent, not at variance, with my upbringing. Furthermore, I cannot for the life of me see that I had any Oedipal problems. Now, Feuer might want to argue that I don't understand myself. If so, the burden of proof is surely upon him.

Likewise, I suspect that most of my fellow students *understood themselves* to be acting out of loyalty to the values of their parents. (Whether or

not they all had Oedipal problems, I do not know.)
I would not want to generalize about all students
on the basis of my few friends of the time, but I
would point out that not one of my friends ever
said anything about having hopelessly repressive
or reactionary parents. All in all, I must say that
those social scientists and political analysts who
stress intergenerational *continuity* between parents and children within a given "class-culture"—
such as Richard Flacks, Kenneth Keniston, Peter
Berger, Robert Coles, Seymour Martin Lipset,
Daniel Moynihan, Edward Banfield, and Midge
Decter—make a lot more sense to me than those
who talk about the Oedipus complex.

THE LIMITS OF PSYCHOANALYSIS

There is another thing about Feuer's employment of psychoanalytic methods which bothers
me, and that is the ease with which they can be
used as "ideological" bludgeons. I have some
doubts about psychoanalysts and psychologists
who presume to analyze their "patients" from
afar—that is, in a nonclinical setting. In 1964,
many were busily certifying that Barry Goldwa-
ter was nuts (although they had never met the
man). Whittaker Chambers, Richard Nixon,
Woodrow Wilson, and many others have received similar treatment. I fear that these exer-
cises are sometimes about as useful as the arguments produced by some theologians to "prove"
the existence of God. That is, they are only con-

vincing to those already convinced.

No doubt, when applied in clinical settings, psychoanalytic methods can often identify the unconscious motivations of particular individuals. But in nonclinical settings, psychoanalytic attempts at explaining behavior are much more hazardous. This is especially so when psychoanalytic methods are applied (nonclinically) to mass phenomena. Such methods then tend to be so speculative that they seem, at times, to carry the odor of unfalsifiability. Since they address themselves to the *unconscious motivations* of masses of anonymous people, one wonders to what extent evidence about *overt* behavior and *articulated* motivations will be permitted to count as counter-evidence or as refutation.

I do not raise this issue in order to be acrimonious, "contrary," or in order to defend the New Left. My intentions are benign. I do not deny that psychoanalytic approaches produce interesting hypotheses. I am not, myself, averse to speculating about the motives of groups of people, although I would insist that speculations not be passed off as "explanations." Once in a while I am even prepared to let down my methodological inhibitions and indulge my political prejudices in order to enjoy a good old-fashioned debunking. But when exploring the irrational sources of hostility to the market system from a rational perspective, we are under an obligation to ensure that our approach to the subject at hand does not carelessly indulge questionable methods of inquiry.

164

At this point it would seem appropriate to focus on the way in which the terms "rational" and "irrational" are employed by Feuer. He acknowledges that there are both rational and irrational sources of opposition to the market system. He seems to regard "rational" motivations as being those of an *economic* character. I presume he would say that if one can show that capitalism is economically inefficient or destructive of the economic well-being of large numbers of people, then one has "rational" grounds for opposing capitalism.

Regarding "irrational" motivations, Feuer has provided us with an impressively long list. I do not understand how *all* of these motivations can be grouped together under the rubric "irrational," especially since Feuer drops the term "neurotic" occasionally, as if to imply that if you're being irrational you just may be neurotic. Regardless of how Feuer chooses to relate neuroses to irrationality, there can be no doubt that Feuer understands irrationality in a pejorative sense. The obviously polemical point Feuer is making is that since there are no viable economic reasons for opposing capitalism today, all current forms of opposition to the market system are unreasonable.

But the irrational motivations Feuer cites are not all of a piece. Some of these motivations are *unconscious,* while others are quite *conscious.* I would want to argue that the *unconscious* motivations (for instance, the response to unconscious aggressive drives, Oedipal problems, infantile fears of numbers, money, competition, and the like) are of quite a different order from the *conscious* motivations (such as convictions that capitalism promotes personal anxiety, hatred of other people, idolization of money and success, that capitalism destroys authority, order, simplicity, and so forth). While I would not dispute the idea that the unconscious motivations are irrational in a pejorative sense, I am uneasy with the placing of *conscious* motivations in the same category.

FROMM, MARCUSE, AND RATIONAL RADICALISM

Although I have no desire to defend the critiques of capitalism offered by Erich Fromm and Herbert Marcuse, I am displeased with the way Feuer deals with their arguments. They argue that capitalism makes people predatory, combative, insecure, possessive, and so on. I am not sure why we should be in such a hurry to label these critiques "irrational." These claims would seem to be, in principle, empirically testable. That is, it would seem to be possible to gather data which would tend to confirm or disconfirm the proposition that capitalist environments encourage people to be more predatory than other environments. I am not asserting that those claims *have been* verified—but simply that, in principle, they could be. Of course, they could be falsified too.

But strangely, Feuer does not even bother to deny these claims. No, he immediately proceeds to

166

an *ad hominem* attack. Instead of challenging the *arguments* of Fromm and Marcuse, he attacks Fromm and Marcuse *themselves,* charging them with being carriers of the "dialectical personality." Although for all I know, Fromm and Marcuse are stark, raving mad, such information would *not suffice* to defeat their arguments.

When Feuer does get around to considering arguments, he still leaves me unsatisfied. He comments on Marcuse's argument that capitalism, by its very nature, does not permit ecological problems to be solved. He says that "irrational, non-logical, non-scientific factors are determining" Marcuse's position because Marcuse completely fails to raise "the question: How has the natural environment fared under the planned socialist economy in the Soviet Union?" Marcuse may be some kind of socialist, but he is certainly no champion of Soviet-style socialism. Surely, Feuer knows that one can be anti-capitalist without thereby being a Soviet apologist, and that Marcuse is, himself, a sharp critic of Soviet socialism.

Unfortunately, Feuer does not consider any of Marcuse's other arguments. He simply proceeds to an indictment of Marcuse, himself, for using language and concepts which supposedly ignite unconscious Oedipal tensions.

Feuer cites Fromm's critique which holds that capitalism encourages people to idolize money, property, things, and so on. Feuer thinks Fromm engages in "more emotional projection than rational analysis." To me, Fromm's critique

167

contains a "rational" component; that is, it seems to be possible to subject his claims about what capitalism does to people to empirical tests.

If for the sake of argument we can agree with Fromm that capitalism does certain things to people, the question becomes one of evaluation —that is: are these things bad? And, even if they are bad, do they outweigh all the good things capitalism does for people? It is at this point that matters begin to get truly "irrational" —but I don't mean that in a pejorative sense. Here we are in the realm of value judgments. Since value judgments are ultimately noncognitive—that is, statements about attitudes, dispositions, matters of taste, and religious convictions —they are to that extent "irrational" or unverifiable. This does not mean that it is impossible to give *reasons* for the values we hold most dear. It simply means that there is usually an irreducible noncognitive dimension to our value judgments. But all of us are forced to make value judgments of this kind from time to time and that is why I am unhappy with the pejorative cast Feuer always gives to the term "irrational."

As for the market system, I suspect that many of its *detractors* would concede that it bestows marvelous economic benefits upon people, but they would argue that these benefits are not worth all the psychological trauma that a competitive society induces. These people *value* (what they consider to be) psychological well-being more than they value economic well-being. I don't see why these people are not entitled to their value judgments.

On the other hand, I suspect that many of capitalism's *defenders* would concede that it promotes personality disorder in certain people, but they would argue that it is a price worth paying for all the economic benefits capitalism showers upon us. These people *value* economic productivity more than increased levels of psychological well-being. That which is being valued here is "economic." This doesn't mean, however, that the judgment made is any less a *value* judgment. I don't know that there is any "rational" hierarchy of values which dictates that we *must* value economic goods over other goods. Some people value economic well-being above all. Other people may value economic well-being, but will sacrifice it for other goods—be it national sovereignty, love of neighbor, love of God, physical health, mental health, or whatever. If these people are to be considered "irrational," then so should the people who value economic well-being above all be considered "irrational." If those who value economic well-being above all are to be considered "rational," then those who value other goods above all should be considered "rational" as well.

I am suspicious of those Marcusean New Leftists who assert *"we* have true consciousness, but *you* have false consciousness." I am as suspicious of those who argue—as Feuer seems to be arguing— *"my* values are rational, but *yours* are irrational."

MANAGING AGGRESSIVE DRIVES

When I think back upon my days as an anti-capitalist radical, I really cannot conceive of myself as
having been a victim of *unconscious* irrational
drives. As I said previously, I was quite conscious
that I was projecting aggressive drives. I was looking for a life full of challenges. The lifestyle of the
rich—indeed, the very ethos of capitalism—
seemed to me to be disgustingly hedonistic, dread-
fully unchallenging. Quite naturally, the idea of
"making it" in the business world never appealed
to me, for what would I do with all the money I
made other than spend it gratifying my frivolous
fancies? No challenges there. (People don't usually
knock themselves out making money in order to
turn right around and give it to charity.) One
might wish to call my quest for a life of challenges
an "irrational" basis for hostility to capitalism. And
yet to me, it made perfect sense—and it still does.
I think Feuer might even be able to sympathize
with me here. For, as he says, man is ultimately a
"problem-seeking animal." But the problem today
is precisely as Feuer puts it: "The excessive, accumulating aggressive energies within him [man]
call for external obstacles which do not exist." As
I see it, the need for external obstacles is just as
pressing as the need for economic well-being—
indeed, the need for challenges intensifies as economic well-being increases (and let us not forget
that economic well-being touches the lives of the
working class as well as other classes). One reason

170

I quit communism was because it became apparent to me in East Germany that Communists were bent on universalizing the lifestyle of Beverly Hills, Hollywood, and Scarsdale. To get rich—either personally or collectively—holds no charms for me.

More generally, it is probably a good thing for the market system that from time to time we go through an economic downturn. Such downturns satisfy—to a small degree—people's need for challenges. No doubt, the "no growth"/"less is better" movement thrives on people's needs to envision a future studded with little challenges. The same might be said of the recent infatuation with Chinese-style permanent revolution, and the current fascination with living "naturally" and venturing out into the wilderness. Personally, I am not attracted to these fads and movements. Nor am I about to argue in favor of economic recession. Yet, I do want to underscore the urgency of the problem of frustrated aggressive drives which Professor Feuer notes in his paper.

I tend to see affluent capitalist society as part of the problem of frustrated aggressive drives, not as part of the solution. It is my conviction that the only constructive, lasting, and ultimately satisfying answer to the quest for a Jamesian "moral equivalent of war" is to be found in traditional religion. Although I cannot discuss the truth claims of religion here, let me just note that religion calls for a life of self-discipline and ceaseless struggle that cannot be relaxed until death. Fortunately, unlike

171

alternate solutions, true religion directs one's aggressions not against another person, not against another nation, race, or class, but against dimensions of oneself. The Christian monk, for example, is called a "soldier of Christ" because he is in perpetual battle with the temptations of his own soul —that is, with himself.

In sum, I would urge defenders of the market system not to be too smug about the economic and supposedly "rational" sources of their convictions, for as someone once said, "Man does not live by bread alone."

FOOTNOTE

1. See: Dale Vree, "Ten Years After the Free Speech Movement: Reflections of a Participant," *Worldview*, 17 (November 1974), pp. 25–30.

7

Capitalism and Its Enemies

Stanley Rothman

There was a period in the 1950s and the early 1960s when it seemed as if a new consensus had been reached in the industrialized non-communist countries at least. To the most influential intellectuals in these countries, Marxism as an ideology had come to seem rather archaic. Besides, it had led to quite authoritarian regimes whenever it had been tried. On the other hand, while "pure" *laissez faire* capitalism was also considered to be outdated, the market system and a modified capitalism were seen to have many virtues. Liberal capitalism had provided an ever-rising standard of living and had preserved individual freedom. On the whole, indeed, it had been associated with rather humane societies.

This view had even come to be held by many intellectuals in the United States who had once been very much on the "left." Liberals and radicals might still attack the "abuses" of the market system, and some of them at one time hoped that

America would eventually evolve into a socialist society, but very few were in a hurry. Really radical attacks on the market system were rare and were largely left to obscure journals of rather limited circulation.

In Europe the picture was somewhat different. In both France and Italy large Communist parties continued to play an important political role and a good many intellectuals were still neo-Marxists; but the communists seemed to have lost their élan and intellectuals were less sympathetic than they had once been. A whole new theory had sprung up which saw Marxism as a product of the infancy of industrialization, as an ideology which reflected the strains of the transition to capitalism. Those intellectuals who advanced this theory predicted the further erosion of Marxist ideology as industrialism advanced in Europe and as the remnants of traditionalism were eliminated.

In England, under the rule of a Conservative government, even the relatively moderate Labor Party was taking a hard look at its doctrine and was retreating somewhat from an earlier commitment to nationalization. Five or more years in office had persuaded many of the Party's leaders that full socialism might not be the answer. And, in Germany, the Christian Democrats were increasing their proportion of the total popular vote on a "free market" platform, while the Social Democrats were in the process of jettisoning much of their Marxist rhetoric.

Even in the communist world, things were look-

174

ing up for free markets. De-Stalinization was under way and some Soviet economists were calling for more attention to be paid to market forces. To be sure, the Chinese were still in a "radical" phase, but, eventually, militancy and rhetoric would erode in the face of reality, or so it was thought.

And, finally, the West had the answers to the problems of the less-developed countries of the "Third World." Conditions were stickier there, for many of these nations seemed committed to radical programs of one sort or another, but, again, this was seen as a transition problem. Provided the advanced industrial nations (especially the United States) offered aid and know-how, the appeals of radicalism would erode in the face of rising standards of living.

How different the intellectual and political scene seems today. During the late 1960s and continuing into the 1970s, business, if not capitalism *per se*, came under increasingly sharp attack in the national media and the *better* universities in the United States, especially among that group of intellectuals which made up the "New Left," but among many "liberals" as well. And while the ferocity of the attack has diminished somewhat, surely American self-confidence in its economic system has been seriously undermined. Further, the generation of the 1960s has now entered the mass media and the universities and both have moved to the left. Courses with radical titles taught by radical professors are among the most popular at the best universities. Radical thought is definitely in vogue if not *de rigueur.*

One must be careful not to exaggerate. The dominant theme in the elite mass media (the major television networks, *Newsweek, Time, The New York Times, The Washington Post*) is "reformist." However, there can be little question of a general lack of sympathy toward the business community and a heightened suspiciousness of it. And, insofar as the "counter-culture" has become institutionalized, American business civilization is portrayed as having produced a semi-mad society, bent on destroying the natural environment.

In Europe, Marxism is once again popular. Indeed, despite reverses, it increasingly dominates the thought of the intellectual community. In France and Italy, Communist parties seriously attempt to become part of the government, and in England and other Western countries the demand for social services and increased equality has created an atmosphere which is less than friendly (to put it mildly) to a free market economy. Fairly sober observers are talking about the loss of élan among European elites and not altogether confident about the survival potential of even mixed economies.

On the other hand, while not without their problems, the Soviet Union and China seem basically stable and powerful. And there are few signs in either country of a shift toward a market economy. Indeed, the argument that the Soviet Union and the United States are converging in the direction of some sort of mixed economy (rather popular in the late 1950s and early 1960s) is no longer heard. And there is little sign, given the power of new generations of computers, that Soviet leadership is going to incorporate substantial market elements in the decision-making process. De-Stalinization may have occurred, but the basic structure of the Stalinist state has been hardly touched, except for the elimination of *arbitrary* terror and the emergence of collective leadership at the top.

What happened? Radicals, liberals, and conservatives, including the contributors to this symposium, have been addressing themselves to these questions during the past five years with increasing frequency. Their answers vary, depending upon ideological predispositions, fields of specialization, and a host of other factors. In what follows I plan to begin with some initial criticisms (or caveats), then to summarize what I conceive to be the major theses of the contributors to this volume. I follow the summaries by certain further, partly critical, remarks, and, finally, I will attempt to offer a synthesis of the insights of the authors (and, indeed, the papers agree on many points and dovetail nicely on others) from my own perspective.

MARKETS WITHOUT CAPITALISM

I have, first, some reservations about "hostility to free markets" as the focus of the symposium. It is at least theoretically possible (although quite unlikely) for a socialist society to rely heavily upon market mechanisms although some may question the label "socialist" in such a case. The contemporary ideological conflict is essentially between those who believe in the viability of liberal capitalism, however modified, and those who wish to replace it with "socialism." To be sure, the term "liberal capitalism" carries with it a number of associations which may cloud some of the issues, but it has the virtue of suggesting the historical context. I will use the terms "liberal capitalism" and "free markets" interchangeably, but it is important to understand what kind of market system we are discussing.

Second, the papers suffer occasionally from what I consider to be a purist perspective. Here I agree with Nathan Glazer. I may be unfair, but there are times when Professors van den Haag, Feuer, and Bauer almost sound as if they believed that every criticism of liberal capitalism reflects "anti-market" hostility. I don't think that any of our participants really hold that view, but the polemical thrust of their essays can leave that impression.

It is, after all, possible to believe in an economy which retains important market elements, while continuing to argue for the state playing a large role in the economic process both in terms of managing the market and in income redistribution. Now, one may argue that the policies which have been accepted even by non-socialist parties in Sweden are self-defeating, but it is wrong, I think, to lump the people who do propose them

178

(unless one has a good deal of evidence) in the same category with Marxist or assorted Maoist or New Left types. One may question whether welfarist or redistributionist policies are "socialist" if they have neither the intention nor the effect of replacing the market by central planning—if production remains private and responsive to private demand and supply.

It is at this point that some of the criticisms of Dale Vree and Nathan Glazer are fairly telling. I have no objection, unlike Dale Vree, to emphasis upon the social psychology of knowledge. The enterprise is a legitimate one. However, it requires special caution.

Finally, some of the analyses on which I am commenting tend to be ahistorical and I think this is a mistake. Once we recognize that we are concerned with liberal capitalism, in other words, a social system based upon private property which relies heavily upon market mechanisms and is closely associated with representative democracy, we must become aware of how short a time, and over how limited a portion of the globe, this system has been dominant or even ascendant. For most of recorded history, most human beings have lived in social and political systems which, while they may have recognized certain rights in property and were willing to allow for some free play of economic forces, considered it entirely right and proper for the major forms of economic activity to be closely controlled by the state or other public agencies.

CULTURAL CONTEXTS OF CAPITALISM

It is quite clear, as Max Weber pointed out in the late 19th century, that liberal "rational bourgeois capitalism" is a European product and, more specifically, a product which has reached its fullest development in nations settled by English Calvinists. It had its beginnings in England and even in Europe itself; it never really took hold in the east or in large parts of the south. In most of Eastern Europe and even in Germany, the state and the state bureaucracy played a very key role in industrialization. Most Eastern European countries never developed an entrepreneurial stratum comparable to that of England or the United States. In fact, with the possible exception of Japan, such a stratum has not developed real strength in any other part of the world. Even in Japan there is some question as to whether the motivations and attitudes of businessmen are really comparable to those of their European counterparts.

Now, this does not necessarily mean that liberal capitalism is an historical oddity which is not exportable. However, the historical and geographic limits of the attitudes and structures associated with it should make one wary about assuming that it is natural and that deviations from it are what have to be explained. One must be open, at least partially, to the notion that the supporters of liberal capitalism have to be explained as much as its enemies. This is true even if one believes that a society based on private property and a relatively free market is probably superior to any current or even conceivable alternatives.

Both Weber and Schumpeter would have found the above suggestion acceptable. Their analyses of the future of liberal capitalism were not all that different. Weber identified the emergence of capitalism and "rationality" with the development of a special kind of ethic based upon a Christian, and more specifically Calvinist, religious sensibility. With the loss of that sensibility he foresaw a number of equally bleak possibilities: 1) bureaucratic socialism or state capitalism which might be both empty and authoritarian; 2) a fall into irrationalism as the outcome of the loss of those non-rational bases underlying a sense of self which Christianity had provided. Weber implied, at least, that the rationalism of the West might, in the end, be self-defeating. Schumpeter took a rather similar view. The rationalizing tendencies of capitalism, the elimination of an aristocracy which had served as a protector of capitalism, and the creation of an alienated intelligentsia were all contributing to the inevitable triumph of socialism. Schumpeter also suggested that a steady state economy (for whatever reason) would weaken the appeal of capitalism. He felt, of course, that a reasonably democratic socialism was at least possible.

REVIEW OF THE ARGUMENTS

Let us turn now to a consideration of our contributors, keeping the above in mind.

181

Ernest van den Haag's discussion of the sources of hostility to the free market is, as everything he writes, both acute and perceptive. But, as he realizes, his essay merely touches on some of the basic issues. Arguing that capitalist development has clearly falsified most of Marx's predictions about progressive impoverishment and has, thus far, provided more people with more consumer welfare than any alternative economic system, van den Haag outlines a number of reasons for the current hostility to free markets:

1. The very success of capitalism has generated discontents among those who are still "poor," despite, or rather because of the fact that the distance between them and the "well-to-do" has diminished. The poor now share much of the outlook of the well-to-do and the "consuming" ambitions. Further, poverty is now seen as a function of social forces rather than as a natural condition. When poverty continues to exist, the social system must be to blame. The rich (or rather their children, who were born rich) share this feeling and are ambivalent about their wealth.

2. The welfare state has created a class of the permanently poor who are resentful of their poverty, but see no need to work because of the very marginal gains which would come from working.

3. Both of the above lead to resentment against the inequalities which are a func-

tion of the market system. Every economic system (including socialist systems) produces inequalities, but socialist systems can promise "utopia" before they come to power and suppress dissent after they come to power. The market system, on the other hand, committed to freedom and having, by its "rationality," subverted the moral legitimacy of its system of inequality, is helpless in the face of criticism. At this point, van den Haag digresses to discuss the justification of inequality. His conclusion is that social inequalities cannot be justified morally, and that, certainly, the type of inequality fostered by a market system cannot be so justified.

The market system, then, can only be defended by pointing to its greater efficiency and creativity, its greater compatibility with freedom, and the fact that alternate systems of (van den Haag says greater) inequality cannot be justified either. In short, while the moral-political case for the market system has flaws, it is stronger than that for alternate realistically conceivable systems. Unfortunately, as van den Haag points out, these are complex arguments unlikely to have mass appeal in the face of utopian politics or strident calls for "justice now." This is especially true because each of us hopes that her or his essential superiority will be realized and that in a system run by an omnipresent parent we will receive our "just" deserts.

4. Anti-capitalist appeals are very persuasive to intellectuals. Many persons choose the "intellectual" professions because the economic rationality of the system is not attractive to them, and because of the power they think they will gain in a planned society. And many now go into the intellectual professions because they can live off their parent's income without any possibility of parental discipline when they engage in generational rebellion.

Drawing upon the experience of rent control in New York, Roger Starr adds to this argument the contention that a major source of hostility to market systems lies in the fact that people do not like to make choices. Underneath much hostility to markets is the desire to escape from freedom to a realm where key life-choices are made for one. While in some sense a critique of van den Haag, Starr's contribution really emphasizes one point which van den Haag has already considered.

Lewis Feuer's analysis of market hostility is couched largely in psychoanalytic terms. His discussion is multifaceted and complex. Feuer points out, correctly I think, that liberal capitalism marked a profound shift from previous social orders in that it redirected primordial aggressive drives to creative purpose. Instead of conquering or plundering other people, men would mix their labor with nature and thus conquer it in the inter-

184

est of "commodious living," to use Thomas Hobbes' felicitous expression.

Despite this fact and the obvious success of liberal capitalism, opposition to free markets has grown in recent years. Feuer notes an underlying irrationality in this opposition, much of which, he argues, is based on the desire not to reform but to aggress, dominate, and control. And he delineates, in the intellectual community, the kind of personality (the "dialectical personality") most prone to such opposition. Such individuals are fixated in generational rebellion. To them the discipline required by work and science is a surrogate for the father who must be destroyed (he cannot be reformed) if the son is to achieve his own goals. These goals point to the creation of a noncompetitive, loving community, in psychoanalytic terms, the possession of the mother. As Feuer argues, I think convincingly, the attacks on capitalism by such intellectuals are often designed to release an underlying hostility to parents, which is projected onto the social system. The attacks reflect a refusal to accept reality and to "grow up." In fantasy life many such individuals desire a society which can be described as that of a "womb with a view," a society in which they can do anything they want without fear of consequences and in which they will never die.

Feuer believes that the generational rebellion of the 1960s was produced by a convergence of neuroses of various kinds and that, by the late 1960s, under the tutorship of gurus like Paul Goodman,

185

Herbert Marcuse, and Erich Fromm, the "dialectical personality" was becoming increasingly dominant. All of this happened, he suggests, because of the very success of capitalism in the United States. Having solved, for large numbers of people, most "real" external problems, capitalism has left many in this generation with no tasks to which they can turn their energies.

The aggression of young people has now no sublimated outlet. Thus, it turns inward, against the system and against parents. This is most often true of intellectually superior children, whose ease in mastering intellectual problems races ahead of emotional maturity. Except for those who come to work in the physical sciences and hence are forced to face reality, such precociousness, suggests Feuer, tends to support infantile narcissism. It is just these kinds of people who have come to populate the universities in a society in which the service sector has grown. Of course their commitment to socialism is reinforced by their feeling that such a society will place them in positions of power. Their dominance in the university has swelled the ranks of the anti-capitalist generation. And, within the camp of the "humanists," it is the least capable who choose the radical path, for it provides them with a rationalization by which they can successfully attack those superior to them. Indeed, in all bureaucratic collectivist societies like the Soviet, the mediocrities rule.

Dale Vree's criticism of Feuer is based on a semi-humorous self-analysis. Vree suggests that his own radicalism was based on conscious hostility to privilege which he picked up from his father rather than from unconscious motives and that his later rejection of the left was based, in part at least, on his perception of the "decadence" of American radicalism. It was also based on the perception that established communist regimes seemed bent on imitating American lifestyles at their worst. Vree criticizes Feuer for his varied usage of the word "unconscious" and for psychological reductionism. He suggests that it is wiser to expend one's energies replying to some of the critiques of capitalism offered by the left.

With Professor Bauer the subject turns to an examination of the anti-capitalist mentality in the less-developed countries. His paper is 1) a criticism of those who argue for the necessity of planning; 2) a critique of those who maintain that the advanced capitalist countries are responsible for the poverty of less-developed countries; 3) a critique of "statist" policies which he regards as a failure; and 4) an examination of the reasons for the popularity of 1, 2, and 3 in the light of what he considers to be obvious errors.

I shall not summarize Professor Bauer's critique of those who blame the market economy or advanced capitalist countries for the "plight" of the less-developed countries, or his criticism of the operation of "statist" economies. His views on these subjects are well known and they are peripheral to his present argument. Suffice it to say, Professor Bauer maintains that it was Western imperialism (and Western investment) that started the less-developed countries on the road to development and that statist economies, because they politicize economic activity, ignore economic realities, and create huge bureaucracies, are less effective than free markets, there as here.

What is the source of the relative predominance of statist doctrines in general and Marxism in particular in the less-developed countries? As Professor Bauer notes, the popularity of both is heavily concentrated among intellectuals, politicians, and administrators (the categories overlap), and is sometimes supported by religious figures. The population at large is not, at least initially, hostile to market systems. Rather, they are propelled in that direction by segments of the elite.

The reasons for elite hostility to capitalism are complex. Professor Bauer lists a large number, six of which seem particularly significant:

First, some of the attitudes of Third World leaders are derived from the teachings of Western economists working for international agencies. Since believers in the importance of planning and of state control dominate the field in these agencies, it is not surprising that such ideas have had so powerful an impact.

Second, intellectuals, administrators, et al., tend to feel both superior to and alienated from ordinary people. They also feel isolated. All of this leads them to believe that it is their duty to determine the course of economic activity and to be particularly attracted to all-embracing creeds which promise reintegration with their fellow countrymen.

Third, foreign aid tends to strengthen the hands of the planners insofar as it goes to governments. It also permits the planners to cover up the failures of planning.

Fourth, Marxism-Leninism and related doctrines enable intellectuals to blame the West (imperialism, neo-colonialism) for problems faced by their own society. Thus, adherence to such doctrines has a self-serving quality which is reinforced by Western guilt feelings. Insofar as the West cries *mea culpa* in the face of charges of imperialism and exploitation and offers increased deference and more aid with each new charge, it is rational and adaptive for the elites in the less-developed countries to adopt radical ideological stances.

Fifth, the traditions of many of these societies are hostile to free economic activity, and it is only natural that this hostility should carry over, especially when industrialization is seen as disruptive of established life-patterns.

And, finally, the business community in most of the less-developed countries is fragmented and nonpolitical in important ways. It does not see that ideas can have important consequences and fails to combat them effectively.

Professor Glazer, concentrating on the role of Western intellectuals, partly supports Professor Bauer, but raises an important question. Glazer argues that until recently the main thrust of economic analysis in the United States was pro-market even if favorable to a certain amount of planning. Why, then, has the younger generation of intellectuals in the West chosen to accept and support neo-Marxist ideas as opposed to the dominant views of their professions? Why, too, have intellectuals in Third World nations preferred to get their economics not from the dominant trends in Western thinking but rather from the "underground" and relatively uninfluential group of radical social theorists? Professor Glazer attempts to answer these questions.

THE LIMITS OF LIBERAL CAPITALISM

Can the essays in this volume be placed within a common framework? I think they can, despite the diversity of approaches and the disparity of the subjects treated. I think they also suggest further areas of research and writing. First, however, we require some additional caveats and clarifications.

I am not at all persuaded by Professors van den Haag or Bauer that free markets are necessarily more effective in producing economic growth and prosperity than are state-dominated economies. The evidence is quite mixed. Despite problems and high costs, both the Soviet Union and China have done rather well as compared, say, to India and many Latin American countries, and so has Cuba. This partly explains the appeal of the statist model. It is true that mixed economies in which the private sector predominates have also done very well in some countries. South Korea, Taiwan, and Japan spring immediately to mind. The point is that the question of efficiency and growth is very complex and very debatable.

This is true even for developed countries. For example, England's problems are not entirely a result of the welfare state in its English form. While I agree that the power of the trade unions and the attempt to create a total welfare state have had a deleterious effect on growth, cultural variables (which partly explain trade union attitudes and the relative lack of dynamism of British entrepreneurs today) are, I suspect, of greater significance. And, more importantly, I see little reason to believe that socialist societies cannot provide the "good things" of life for their citizens. Contrary to the views expressed by Professors Bauer and van den Haag, I believe that socialist societies may be less efficient in some ways than liberal capitalist societies, but they avoid some elements of waste which are endemic to such societies.

Second, it is far from clear that the distribution of income in socialist societies will necessarily be more *unequal* than in liberal capitalist societies. Reliable data are hard to come by, but the best I have seen suggests that the distribution of income in Cuba and China is more equal than in the United States. Income spread in the Soviet Union is about the same except at the margins, though the distribution of rewards is rather different. (In the Soviet Union, top salaries go to high-level military and party personnel.) If the Soviet Union does give an indication of the direction in which socialist societies are likely to go, I suspect that socialist and capitalist societies do not differ substantially in this area.[1]

It seems to me that the strongest arguments for liberal capitalism are: 1) It is more likely to be associated with representative democracy than is socialism; 2) It is less likely to become over-bureaucratized, with all the evils that entails; 3) It encourages individualism in general and individual creativity in particular; and 4) It relies upon and encourages individual rationality and a sense of self. While I regard all of these features of liberal capitalist market economies as virtues, they can be, as van den Haag, Feuer, and Starr have pointed out, a real source of weakness.

I regard the essays in this volume as very important. I noted earlier Dale Vree's suggestion that the sociology/social psychology of knowledge is not the most legitimate enterprise. I disagree. An understanding of the nonrational sources of attitudes is significant in itself as an aid to understanding historical development. Further, the attempt to bring to light such nonrational elements may serve to increase the rationality with which we can deal with events. The uncovering of motives is no substitute for rational argument about alternatives. However, all of our contributors have engaged in such argument at great length. This volume has a somewhat different purpose.

So much for criticism. What about the possibilities of synthesis? We can achieve this, I think, by starting in reverse order of my summary and discussing first anti-market feeling in Third World nations. In doing this, let me stress again what I said in my introductory remarks. Liberal capitalism as a set of ideas emerged out of a particular cultural matrix. It was derived from societies which were heir to Greek, Roman, and Jewish themes as fused in Latin Christendom. It was a matrix which emphasized, even in Catholicism, rational understanding of nature (including the downplaying of magic and mysticism), individualism, and a kind of universalism which broke through clan and ethnic ties, thus permitting the establishment of commercial contractual activity even before capitalism. It is true that, in the 19th century, Whig historians saw the Catholic Church as antithetic to liberal individualism, science, and capitalist industrialization. They were, however, highly ethnocentric. In a comparative context, it is clear that Western culture paved the way for such a development and that Calvinist Protestantism provided, as it were, an additional factor at a critical point, which enabled a number of countries to modernize first.

In Europe, the cultures of some countries were, for a variety of reasons, far more compatible with capitalist development than others. The United States, for example, born a Calvinist nation, and lacking a feudal tradition, carried within itself from the beginning the seeds of an almost ideal-type liberal capitalist civilization. For somewhat different reasons, Germany, once it turned to modernization, was able to rely upon a population whose Lutheran Christian heritage (with a stress on self-control and discipline) yielded a passion for meticulousness and order which carried liberal capitalism rapidly forward.

Thus, the breakthrough to capitalism depended upon energies directed into a practical activity, with aggression controlled or sublimated, ego strength emphasized (if I may use psychoanalytic terminology), and individual creativity stressed in ways that were not found elsewhere. As I noted earlier, nowhere else in the world did an indigenous bourgeoisie emerge comparable to the Western type. In Japan and other cultures in the Confucian cultural sphere, it is clear that, once opened by the West, certain cultural features have encouraged rapid industrialization. Even in Japan, however, the motives underlying the kind of hard work that has yielded rapid growth were other than those of the West and still are to a considerable extent. This is not to deny the presence in many societies of individuals and groups which have shared some of the characteristics of the Western bourgeoisie, but such groups have never become culturally dominant.

THIRD WORLD COUNTRIES AND CULTURES

Liberal capitalism and industrialization were brought to non-European parts of the world by example and by conquest. Here, I must disagree, in part, with Professor Bauer. I have no doubt that

194

the West (as even Marx pointed out) played an important role in weakening traditional social orientations and in providing an example of new ways of doing things. I agree, too, that Western imperialism was not nearly as exploitative as most traditional imperialisms. But exploitative to some degree it was. More importantly, it imposed upon non-European intellectuals a sense of inferiority which they are still attempting to overcome. Indeed, as Levinson has argued, the adoption of radical Marxism by Chinese intellectuals can be seen, in part, as an attempt to re-establish the superiority of their society by adopting the "most advanced" Western position.[2] In attacking capitalism, they also get back at the West for both psychic and physical harm. Structurally similar themes, incidentally, were found to a lesser extent in Germany when she was attempting to find her place in the world and in Russia during the intellectual ferment of the 19th century. Arab, African, and Latin American socialists, too, all urge the superiority of their own cultures when combined with advanced Western positions.

It is this psychic hurt and desire to establish their equality with (or superiority to) Europeans which *partially* explains the attractiveness of more radical Western ideologies (critical of the West and "blaming" the West) to intellectuals in the Third World. I agree, in part, with Glazer that, until the 1960s, when the picture began to change rapidly, Asian, African, Latin American, and Arab intellectuals sought out radical "progressive doctrines"

195

which were not explicitly dominant in the United States.[3]

But certainly another variable has to do with the very lack of an indigenous "Protestant" type middle class. Under such circumstances it has been natural for the political elite in the various less-developed countries to feel that the task of industrializing depends upon them—since they cannot expect the proper attitudes to well up from below —and that they must be the ones to change their societies. Again, the Third World is not alone in this. During the 19th century, industrialization in almost every East European state from Germany to Russia was initiated by the state and its bureaucracy. In some of these countries, an entrepreneurial class finally did emerge. In others, Communist revolutions and takeovers precluded that possibility.

Of course, all of the other factors rightly mentioned by Professor Bauer, including the authoritarian tradition of pre-existing cultures (and the lack of individualism), the denigration of commercial activity, and sheer self-interest, are important. But the cultural matrix and the sense of being in a hurry (which always encourages large-scale planning) plays, I would argue, along with hostility toward Europe and its legatee, the United States, a very great role.

I would just add one more factor. In Europe, the breakdown of traditional *external* controls over behavior associated with the shift to modern society involved their replacement by inner controls

196

(a strong superego) derived from Christian sources.[4] Individualism, as it emerged in the world, operated within the framework of certain very important restraints. These have been gradually breaking down in the West. In most non-European societies they never were present. With change coming from the outside and destructive of the indigenous culture, Western liberal ideas often seem to produce almost instant anomie. It is for this reason that many in non-European countries see liberal individualism (and the free markets associated with it) as a source of decay in their own societies and, I should add, increasingly in the West. Little wonder that they shy away from it and try to maintain, albeit in "modern" forms, a collective conscience and order that in many ways looks suspiciously similar (despite a collectivist orientation) to traditional American Calvinism. This is why some American radicals of the New left variety (as well as various Bohemians) finally found Cuba, Russia, and China so unattractive. The emphasis in all of these countries has been on work, order, and discipline. And dominant communist elites are almost invariably opposed to such manifestations of Western "decadence" as homosexuality, modern art, and even uncontrolled heterosexuality.

Of course, at least some "puritan" radicals from the West found just these themes attractive in the early days of the Soviet and Chinese experiments and have been disillusioned by the fact that the Soviet Union and Eastern Europe, especially, are

197

opening up a bit. Dale Vree at one stage in his transition, so he tells us, had just that reaction.

The utopian elements in Marxism-Leninism have certainly appealed to Third World intellectuals for the reasons cited by Professor Bauer and others. However, they are not alone in being attracted to such ideals, and this brings us to the advanced industrial, liberal capitalist nations, primarily the United States.

DISSENT IN THE UNITED STATES

Except in the United States, liberal capitalism never has had a universally good press, even in European countries. Lest we forget, during the 1930s the European intelligentsia was talking of the end of capitalism and was persuaded that either fascism or communism was the wave of the future. It was America's victory in World War II, the prosperity of the postwar period (primarily that of America again) and the impossibility of ignoring the crimes of Stalin that resulted in a decline in the intellectual dominance of the left during the 1950s. Indeed, the United States in the 1950s became a model for European youth and for substantial segments of the intellectual community. Many of them (despite a good deal of ambivalence) felt that the future of their own societies was to become more like the United States, and during the whole of the 1950s they were importing large segments of American culture, from its social science to its music.

And, as noted earlier, during the 1950s leading American intellectuals, while reformist, did not seem anti-system. We are back to the question raised at the beginning of this essay. What brought about the change?

The precipitating factors are quite obvious, namely the race issue and the war in Vietnam. Somehow the failure to solve the one and our involvement in the other became tied up with a critique of capitalism itself, as well as of many other American institutions and patterns of behavior. And there can be little doubt that American self-doubt and self-criticism, relayed to Europe via television and the cinema, served to encourage the student left there and the general revival of radical intellectual orientations.

This has happened before. After all, during the 1930s a segment of the American intelligentsia moved to the left, giving up on American institutions in the face of economic depression. The 1970s are different only because: 1) The intellectual class is much larger; and 2) Given national media and a national media elite, centered in New York and Washington, which is quite sensitive to current intellectual fashions, intellectuals are much more influential than they once were. If this is the case, the solution to the race issue might restore faith in our institutions, which have suffered only a temporary decline in the face of specific problems. The above is not a particularly optimistic prognosis, because the race issue is perhaps the most intractable problem the United States has ever faced. It is, however, much more optimistic than those offered by the authors here or by scholars like Daniel Bell.[5] For while they might agree that the precipitating causes are as I have described them, they see a much deeper malaise. Professors van den Haag and Feuer agree with each other on many of these underlying factors and I agree with them. Again, however, I should like to place these in context.

I take as my starting point, with Professor Feuer, that human beings have both affectional and aggressive needs; and that rationality (in psychological terms, ego strength) is easier to destroy than to create, given the power of unconscious drives; finally, that human beings, taken as a whole, need some kind of religious sensibility (it can be otherworldly or secular) in order to be able to face the inevitability of decay and death.

I have already argued that the growth of ego strength (rationality) in European history was based upon the strength of internal controls (a strong superego) derived from Christian sources. And yet, as both van den Haag and Feuer agree, this growth in rationality has weakened the foundations upon which it was built, for liberal capitalism is beset by a series of contradictions. Feuer and van den Haag list several, but others may be added. The emphasis on "commodious living" is transmuted into the desire to consume everything one can and erodes traditional emphases on the need for self-discipline and hard work. The emphasis on individualism and individual responsibility is eroded by rationalistic psychological theories (the products of Western rationalism) which suggest that it is the larger society which is responsible for our ills rather than our own actions. That same rationality undermines the religious sensibility which gave individuals the courage to make their own choices and to accept the limits of human existence.

The speed with which these contradictions have undermined existing cultural patterns is, in part, a function of technology and in part a function of the growing power of the "knowledge" stratum produced by liberal capitalist affluence. This stratum consists of the most cosmopolitan types, those exemplifying in themselves most fully the results of the contradictions noted above.

Most of the reasons for this have been outlined by Professors Feuer and van den Haag, and, indeed, although they have been little studied, there is a good deal of evidence that the choice of profession by future intellectuals is often dictated by their hostility to the existing culture. It is the more radical students in the universities and colleges who are most likely to choose teaching or journalism as a career. And the courses they take in college reinforce such attitudes, as does the professional socialization they eventually receive. This socialization also gives them the training which enables them to rationalize their hostility to the culture under the guise of social reform and

201

humanitarianism. This is even more true of those entering such professions now than it was ten years ago.[6]

Professor Feuer is largely correct in this description of their modal personality. My own study of radical students, employing projective tests, indicates that they are characterized by strong power drives, little concern for people as people, high levels of generalized hostility, and a considerable amount of narcissism.[7] Not all persons in the knowledge professions can be characterized in this way, and the evidence does not seem to bear out Professor Feuer's suggestion that the primary sources of such personality characteristics are always Oedipal. But these are minor points.

Such persons fall prey easily to millennial ideologies, because as "secular intellectuals" they need religious substitutes and because such ideologies provide a weapon against the larger society. And, given their control over the means of communication, they spread their malaise to the more traditional groups within the society, including the working class. This is especially true of television which, as Michael Robinson has demonstrated, has a unique capacity to erode faith in the economic and political system.[8]

A FAILURE OF NERVE

Professor Glazer is certainly correct in suggesting that the last generation of academics (and other professionals) was not as radical as all that. The real radicals *were* few in number. However, the failure of academics and other professionals to effectively resist the counter-culture of the 1960s and their cautious sympathy with much of it indicates that it resonated with something in them. The older generation was simply more sublimated. Their children, and, as a number of studies have indicated, the elite of the counter-culture were their children, were often acting out the fantasies of their parents. This was a form of generational rebellion, but not exactly the kind that Feuer suggests. And it is these same intellectuals who join international agencies or otherwise convey to Third World intellectuals the idea that Western capitalism is exploitative and should be transcended, even as they convey the same arguments to a new generation of students.

In the face of all this, entrepreneurs in advanced capitalist countries, like their counterparts in the less-developed countries, are at a loss. They have by and large been action- and achievement-oriented persons with little comprehension of the power of ideas spread by intellectuals and they find it difficult to combat them effectively.[9]

Everything I've said is quite supportive of the points raised by van den Haag, Feuer, and Bauer, although I have added a few things. If we differ at all it is only because I have suggested that the nonrational elements in an anti-market position may be more natural to human beings than the modal personality required to support liberal capitalism. And, indeed, their own arguments suggest that this is true.

So the liberal capitalist nations of the West are facing rather difficult times. For to all of the above must be added a shift of the balance of power in the world away from them. There is every reason to believe that most of the Third World will grow increasingly hostile to the West, and will choose socio-political orders which involve large elements of state control. This does not necessarily mean that Western Europe and America are lost. Conceivably they could remain islands of "rationality," and of mixed, though predominantly market, systems for some time, even in a non-market world. This would require, however, a kind of "nerve" which may be lacking.

One's final view, therefore, must be rather pessimistic. Given the unlikelihood of a revival of traditional Western religious sensibilities, our only hope would seem to lie in heightened rationality. Insofar as the authors have attempted, in this volume, to uncover some of the nonrational sources of hostility to free markets, they have made a contribution to this effort.

By their own admission, however, the chances that the effort will bear much fruit are not terribly great. In my more negative moments I am almost persuaded that liberal capitalism has indeed been an historical oddity that, like an earlier experiment in democracy (Athens at the height of its glory), always carried within it the seeds of its own decay.

FOOTNOTES

1. For a discussion see David Lane, *The End of Inequality?* (Penguin Books, 1971). Excellent discussions of aspects of income distribution in the Soviet Union and China respectively are: Mervyn Matthews, "Top Incomes in the USSR: Towards a Definition of the Soviet Elite," *Survey,* Summer 1975, pp. 1–27, and Martin King Whyte, "Inequality and Stratification in China," *The China Quarterly,* December 1975, pp. 684–711.

2. Joseph R. Levinson, *Modern China and Its Confucian Past* (New York: Anchor Books, 1964).

3. It should be pointed out, however, that such doctrines had far more currency in France and England, and a larger proportion of Third World intellectuals were educated in those countries than in the United States. Since many Third World leaders received their education in the 1940s and even in the 1930s, they were in both England and France at a time when Marxism and related doctrines had yet to experience the decline which occurred in the 1950s.

4. See Fred Weinstein and Gerald M. Platt, *The Wish to be Free* (Berkeley: University of California Press, 1969).

5. Daniel Bell, *The Cultural Contradictions of Capitalism* (New York: Basic Books, 1976).

6. By and large there are very few scholarly studies on the sociology and psychology of the "knowledge" professions. Everett Carll Ladd and S. M. Lipset did complete a massive study of teachers, *The Divided Academy* (New York: McGraw Hill, 1975), but there is nothing comparable on journalists.

7. See Stanley Rothman et al., "Ethnic Variations in Student Radicalism," in Severyn Bialer, ed., *Sources of Contemporary Radicalism* (Boulder, Colorado: The Westview Press, 1977). (A fuller report of my study will appear as a volume, *The*

Radical Impulse, to be published by Oxford University Press.)
I have also begun, with several other colleagues, a study of the
national media elite, following the pattern of my student
study.

8. Michael J. Robinson, "American Political Legitimacy in an
Era of Electronic Journalism: Reflections on the Evening
News," in Richard Ader, ed., *Television as a Social Force* (New
York: Praeger, 1975), pp. 97–139.

9. The more "liberal" of them hold to the rather naïve view
that social scientists are "objective," and expect the "real"
knowledge of business will improve its image. They then set
up foundations run by social scientists and are shocked and
dismayed by the studies which issue forth. This is far from
surprising given the domination of the social science community by those who consider themselves to be quite liberal, if
not radical. For these and other reasons the great majority of
the hundreds of social science studies that appear each year
are based on assumptions which frequently (and by definition)
support negative views of the system.